TRISTAN GOOLEY is a writer, navigator and explorer. He is the author of *The Natural Navigator* and *The Natural Explorer*. He has written for a host of publications including the *Sunday Times*, the *New York Times*, the *FT* and *Geographical Magazine*.

Tristan has led expeditions in five continents, climbed mountains in Europe, Africa and Asia, sailed small boats across oceans and piloted small aircraft to Africa and the Arctic. He is the only living person to have both flown solo and sailed singlehanded across the Atlantic and is a Fellow of the Royal Institute of Navigation and the Royal Geographical Society.

Tristan has appeared on TV and radio programmes in the UK and internationally. Visit his website at: www.naturalnavigator.com

THE SCHOOL OF LIFE is dedicated to exploring life's big questions: *How do we find fulfilling work? Can we ever understand our past? Why are relationships so hard to master? If we could change the world, should we?* Based in London, with offices around the globe, The School of Life offers classes, therapies, books and other tools to help you create a more satisfying life. We don't have all the answers but we will direct you towards a variety of ideas from the humanities – from philosophy to literature, psychology to the visual arts – guaranteed to stimulate, provoke, nourish and console.

D0785811

By the same author:

The Natural Navigator

The Natural Navigator Pocket Guide

The Natural Explorer

How to Connect with Nature
Tristan Gooley

MACMILLAN

First published 2014 by Macmillan
an imprint of Pan Macmillan, a division of
Macmillan Publishers Limited

Pan Macmillan
20 New Wharf Road, London N1 9RR
Basingstoke and Oxford
Associated companies throughout the world
www.panmacmillan.com

ISBN 978-0-230-76807-9

9 8 7 6 5 4 3 2 1

A CIP catalogue record for this book is
available from the British Library.

Cover design by Marcia Mihotich
Typeset by seagulls.net
Printed and bound by CPI Group (UK) Ltd,
Croydon, CR0 4YY

Contents

I. Introduction

There are many people who will cajole you to take an interest in nature because they see this as a necessary part of a broader environmental goal. I am not one of them and this book is not part of that benevolent drumbeat. Of course everybody wants to live in a sustainable environment, in the same way that nobody of right mind wants war. Some people are more passionate about it than others, but no sane person likes to see the planet irrevocably harmed.

In this book I am imploring you to connect with nature for a different reason. This reason is that it is the best possible deal out there. A strong connection with nature will give you a much more interesting experience, every minute you spend outdoors. That is one side of the deal. The other side is that this connection will make you a more interesting and effective person. I know that is a bold, if not arrogant statement, but I do mean it. Have you ever found yourself talking to somebody who is so engrossed in the practical details of life that you find it hard to connect with them? Perhaps the person who talks about their plans for developing their property without relenting? Or the one who knows the cost of everything and the value of nothing?

Have you ever lost interest in somebody because they are so enthralled by their own philosophical view of an issue that they cannot see the real world around them? I'm thinking of the person who corners you to discuss problems in the developing world, oblivious to the fact there is a young child playing with a sharp knife next to them.

The joy of discovering a deep connection with nature is that it allows each of us to see each living thing, object and idea within its own intricate network. It allows us to view things in the most practical and philosophical way simultaneously. There is no other field that I am aware of that does this. We can look at a plant as a source of food, and as a key to appreciating a moment in time – at the same time.

The desire to connect with nature is not commonplace. Most people remain oblivious to the sounds of the birds all around them. They can ignore the most exquisite form of a wildflower and fail to find any beauty in the insect by their feet. 'Surely,' we might hear them say, 'only those geologists who have opted out of society can find a rock interesting.' This is the ordinary view. It is a view held by a lot of people who would be happy to have more interesting lives.

Since you are reading this book, you take the extraordinary view. You either suspect or already know that feeling a connection with nature has the potential to be an exciting and meaningful experience. Perhaps you have a desire to rediscover a lost connection: if we go back far enough we all find there was once a bond. It is found for many in memories of childhood, but we can be certain of finding it by going back further still, to our ancestors.

Later in the book I will argue that the stimulation a full connection with nature can bring to each person is life-enhancing to the point where it changes who we are. However, there are a few steps to take before that small leap and in Part II of the book I will introduce each of these. In Part III we will explore each step more fully and in Part IV we will look at the importance of understanding the concept of time in nature. The fifth and final part of the book covers the wild philosophical places these steps can lead to.

II. The Ground Ahead

1. Getting Ready

'The obvious is usually profoundly significant.'
(EDWARD O. WILSON)

What does it mean to feel a connection with nature?

It means gaining an insight into the most important network there ever has been and ever will be. It means becoming aware of our relationship with this network. It means expecting a fascinating and enriching experience each time we step outside. And it means embarking on a journey that leads towards the realization that every single thing that we have found interesting up to this point in our lives has its roots in this network we call nature. Health, business, politics, sport, sex, violence and culture: all subsets of nature.

A connection with nature allows us to see the roots that sustain and explain everything around us. The interest we find in a place is intimately tied to the history of that place and how far back we look. Many people focus on what has taken place during the past week, or two hundred years, but we can look back millions of years if we choose to. Politicians may like to warm themselves by focusing on the belief that they are arguing in the Houses of Parliament because they are very important representatives of the People. They only see the last pages of the book; if they flicked back to earlier chapters they would see that they are just *Homo sapiens*, a species that needs a lot of water to thrive and migrates towards rivers to form colonies in places like Westminster. Big Ben might be thought of as the plumage of that one peculiar species.

In 1943, the American psychologist Abraham Maslow proposed a theory based around a human hierarchy of needs. He suggested that healthy development follows a sequence that progresses from the most basic needs, like food and shelter, towards more complex emotional ones, like respect and self-esteem. It is an idea that is mirrored in the steps necessary to form a deep connection with nature.

Our ancestors must have subconsciously appreciated that a discussion about self-esteem was a low priority if they were starving and suffering from frostbite. Busy, 'sophisticated' modern humans allow themselves to believe that these earlier, lower stages in the hierarchy are in the past, of little relevance to our lives today. But this is a mistake; if we are looking to make a profound connection with our environment we cannot start at the top. Some of the first areas to explore are the practical ways that we can reconnect with nature.

For the majority of us it is possible to experience a deep sense of joy in *doing* something new. This desire for novelty may no longer be vital in terms of survival, but it is essential if we want to think differently. This is because there are some basic actions that can bypass our modern and artificial obstacles to thinking. It does not take a huge change in lifestyle to achieve this joy; small actions introduced to a modern routine can have the desired effect. The simple act of using the sun or moon to prevent yourself from becoming disorientated as you drive to a new friend's home, for instance, is a more important experience than many might have guessed.

Sheltering from the wind in a hollow, eating wild berries or curing an ailment with a leaf are no longer necessary physically; we can buy products to overcome these challenges instead. But to achieve a connection with nature they are wonderful early steps. Ludicrously simple acts with obvious consequences can offer surprising philosophical rewards. Walking towards the sound of water gurgling in a stream when thirsty, instead of thinking about a tap or bottle, can open up new thought patterns. A basic new action can blow away some of the sophistries that get in the way of profound insight. This is an idea that has been central for Buddhists for centuries, not least the Zen and Shugendo movements, but which remains important to all of us, regardless of our personal religion or philosophy. That is the whole point of *doing* it.

New actions inevitably lead to new experiences, and this novelty kicks our senses out of the slump induced by routine. This in turn raises our levels of awareness. One of the peculiar consequences of starting to notice new things is that we cannot help but notice how little we have been noticing hitherto.

Once we notice something that until now has slipped past us, our minds are likely to develop a voracious appetite for more. We will not be satisfied with a morsel, but find ourselves urging our senses on to devour all the things out there that we have overlooked. And unlike so many urges to binge, this desire is healthy. Heightened awareness is one of the few mind-altering 'substances' which lends itself to excess without redress.

The way to satisfy this craving is to get to know our senses and then work with them, tuning them, giving them a good workout and then unleashing them on new areas. Ask someone, ideally someone you trust, to lead you on a blindfolded walk. Then remove the blindfold and attempt to draw the landscape you walked through. The act of using your senses in a new way and drawing, whether or not you consider yourself an artist, will lead to a new sensory awareness. If that all sounds like too much effort to start with, then just try walking into an open outdoor space and lying on the ground for ten minutes. The required effort-levels don't get much lower.

Our senses soon reward their new fitness. We start to notice new beauty. Things that once hid behind the great veil of busyness stand out. It is as though a mist has cleared. We see shapes and colours that can't possibly have been around us all along. Can they?

Our senses repay us in so many surprising ways. We become aware of the way things change and react. It is so much easier to connect with someone or something that reacts to you. You're thicker-skinned than most if you do not react at all when somebody comments on your clothing, and amazingly scientists have proved that even plants react to the clothes we wear.

Plants react to colours. For example, if we are dressed in blue we can change the way a plant grows, while if we wear red we will influence its timekeeping. The process by which plants grow towards light is called phototropism and is only influenced by blue light. Red light, on the other hand, influences photoperiodism, which governs the plant's sensitivity to the time of year. The changes in a plant that result from our choice of clothing colour may be imperceptible to us, but the knowledge that they are reacting can change the way we think about them.

The Glorious War

As our senses fuel a growing awareness of our surroundings, something strange happens. A new dynamism becomes apparent. This nice wallpaper that we have been calling 'nature' and ignoring for ages is no longer quite so easy to ignore. Why? Because we find ourselves drawn into the conflict raging all around us.

Conflict is one of the few guaranteed ways of luring us into a subject. We are programmed to find conflict interesting. Movies, soap operas and boxing matches all rely on conflict to keep bums on seats. Nature is a box-office winner for those who notice and understand the conflict inherent in it.

Those who are determined to find nature uninteresting are unaware of nature's hand of cards. Nobody goes into a game of poker with someone who can summon aces at will. Nature's trump card is that we are programmed, by nature, to find conflict fascinating, and nature is conflict. No card sharp can beat that hand. Almost every living thing is permanently engaged in a battle of survival. It is the longest-running, highest-budget, most compelling drama that has ever been staged. There are recurrent themes, as there are in all good dramas, but no commercial breaks, no repeats and no cheap seats.

Something and Violence

Why do sex and violence get paired and then blamed for impairing the minds of young people via computer and TV screens? Partly because kids gravitate towards these two phenomena: they make for irresistible stories. It is not just rubber-necking drivers on roads who find carnage magnetic. Have you ever noticed how kids can't resist pausing by death? I walked in the woods with one of my sons the other day and found him lagging behind. When I retraced my steps to see if he was okay, I found him hypnotized by a dead stoat beside the path. A small motionless corpse held his attention in a way that would make Nintendo shareholders salivate.

Violence we know as the final dance of conflict, but sex is equally important to our psyches. Our species is not alone in finding sex of overwhelming interest at times. The instruction manual that Darwin found threaded through nature reads something like this:

Step 1: Find conflict and sex of interest, or die, lonely and then extinct.

Step 2: Make sure you understand Step 1.

That is not a pretty flower you are looking at. It's a sex machine, whoring itself to the bees. How can something so pretty be so wanton! The intrigue grows when we realize that some vibrant colours attract while others repel.

Poisons have failed in their task if they are ingested; it is too late to deter something that has already eaten you. And so organisms warn predators that trouble is in store with bright colours and extreme contrast. Predators soon learn that these combinations make for a poor meal or worse. We learn to make similar associations too. The greater the contrast and the brighter the colours in our road signs, the more likely there is danger ahead. Dull brown and a little white:

something harmless, like a tourist attraction. Lots of bright yellow and some black: potential hazard, like a low bridge.

Some of the most admirable creatures use colour and contrast for both sexual allure and violent repellence. The peacock butterfly is instantly recognizable to mates, but is also able to deter predators. One flex of its wings, and 'eyes' appear on its back, and the rodent predator sees an arch-enemy owl and scuttles away in a panic.

The Venus flytrap is one of the most famous plants in the world, loved by many, not least kids, and abhorred by a few too. But nobody finds it dull on first meeting. 'A plant that springs a trap shut and murders its victims in an acid bath, you say? Tell me more.' Well, okay, if you insist. The *flytrap* part of the name comes, logically, from its habit of trapping flies. The *Venus* part comes from the lewd imagination of eighteenth-century naturalists like John and William Bartram, who thought they saw a likeness of the female genitalia in the form of *Dionaea muscipula*.

Is that bright colour trying to lure something into bed, or warning of a poison that will kill? Butterflies and fungi. Sex and violence.

A Unique Experience

New awareness leads us to notice time in a fresh way. Time is shy and likes to remain concealed for half a lifetime or more. It is no coincidence that those whose time has been called, those who battle a terminal illness, are the people who report the most intense awareness of their surroundings and the passing of time. But we need not wait for such a predicament to stop, look and listen. An interest in nature is a philosophical pension. The sooner you start investing, the greater and longer the rewards. Did I mention that it doesn't cost anything?

A path you thought you knew now sounds different underfoot, and is slippery with fallen leaves. The light is different too and a new strong smell of decay engulfs you. Sights, sounds and smells mutate with the months. There are the most extraordinary fresh-air calendars to be found on each walk. The Ongee, the indigenous people of the Andaman Islands, use a scent calendar. As each flower blossoms and gives its scent to the forest air, that is the smell that comes to define the time of year.

The clock that cannot be bought, the one that mocks those ineffectual coils and springs, is tick-tocking all around. If we return at a later date to a spot we have visited, it will be a very different place. The more we notice, the more obvious it becomes that it is impossible to return to the same spot twice. And strange new sensations crowd in around.

If we stay out past sunset, we will notice that certain star constellations hide for much of the year: Orion is a winter constellation, Scorpius a summer one. The night sky holds other regular visitors who appear as promised and then disappear for a whole year. If we are sensitive to these changes in the sky, then they come to be closely associated with the seasonal changes on the ground and our own habits. The gardening writer Katherine Swift, for example, likes to welcome the Perseid meteor shower after jam-making in August.

More excitingly, and alarmingly, it is impossible even to return to the same place within a single day. The daily changes that shape each place are dramatic, but take greater levels of awareness to unlock and so go unnoticed by almost everyone. As the flowers react to the angle of light and the sun makes its way across the sky, whole fields change colour. When my neighbour has sown linseed, the field I know best turns from a moody mauve in the morning to an ebullient purple at lunchtime. Each and every day, birdsong is marking out a soundscape that shifts west as the earth turns and we find ourselves standing on a music box that needs no winding.

The world around us is morphing; it is a shape-shifter. Colours, smells and sounds swirl through daily and annual patterns, putting on displays then disappearing with promises to return in new clothes. There is the regularity of a solar drum behind all the changes, but this regularity passes through the individual kaleidoscope that is our locality. Time makes both sense and a delightful madness of each place and moment. The only certainty is that you will only get one opportunity to experience each scene exactly the way it is. It will be different if you return in ten months or ten minutes.

Time is not content to limit its power to conducting the changes in the landscape all around us, and one of its delicious tricks is to slip in through our ears and sculpt our thoughts and senses. We all have individual chronotypes, which is just a scientific way of saying that we are subject to our own daily ups and downs. Some have energy in the mornings, the larks, some in the evenings, the owls, and many of us like to throw coffee, chocolate and stronger things at these tides in an effort to manipulate them. Our experience of the world is deeply subjective.

Each day our sleep patterns, blood-sugar levels and hormones dramatically repaint the scenes we see. Psychologists are building a better and more bizarre understanding of the world as we see it. In a lecture I gave at the Royal Geographical Society, I showed the audience a photograph of a pile of bananas and asked them to quickly shout out the colour they first saw. 'Yellow!' they cried at first. Then, 'No, White.' The photo was black and white. The world is not always as it seems and time, like shapes, can trick us.

The Banana Skin and the Great Network

As we set out to build a stronger connection, we need to beware an early trap. It is very hard to find nature interesting if you are bundling all of it into one lot. This is the biggest risk early on.

Nature is not one big pile. Plants set some people on fire and douse the enthusiasms of others. Some dedicate much of their life to the study of an individual insect species while others recoil at any creepy-crawly they see. The pioneering American planter of apple trees, John Chapman, felt it wrong to ride a horse or chop down a tree. He was so cross when he accidentally stepped on a worm that he punished his own foot by throwing away its shoe. Nature is diverse. People are diverse. Each to their own. And footwear is optional.

It is not just feathers and leaves and those millions of living organisms that stimulate intrigue and obsession. The eminent metallurgist Cyril Smith was colour-blind. He formed his own fascination and bond with nature by learning to appreciate the intricate patterns in metal alloys. Smith became sensitive to the 'swirls, filigree, and banding' that each metal offered his senses. The biologist Edward O. Wilson has gone so far as to claim that the love of machines is but a specialist form of nature-loving. Jeremy Clarkson is therefore a naturalist. He has been called many things, but a naturalist? Well, let's try petrol-head instead. Petrol is refined oil, which is derived from decomposed zooplankton and algae. Clarkson may not be a naturalist in the common understanding of the word, but he is a zooplankton-head.

In time we come to appreciate that the tiny part of nature's spectrum that lures us in at first – perhaps the birds, the orchids, the colour of sand; who knows, except you? – is intimately connected to one or two other parts. We come to know those other parts by association. A best friend's friend becomes a friend, enemy or lover with time.

Whatever first draws you in, there will come a moment when it becomes clear that its close connections in turn have their own connections. This is the exhilarating moment when we realize that everything is connected. It is something that we need to experience ourselves; merely being told about nature's interconnectedness, here or anywhere else, can prompt you to look for it, but it cannot recreate the effect of experiencing it. For all who take the time to find it, there comes a giddy second when the pieces suddenly fly together in a dizzying vortex of geology, biology, ecology and many other words ending in 'ology'. But, thankfully, this experience takes place without the words themselves attached. Our attempts to label things don't make the beauty or our experience of it. They can help or hinder us in our attempts to find it, but they form the map, not the territory, and are far from the extraordinary experiences to be found within it.

Our senses might reveal an animal, which can tell us something about the plants with which it shares its habitat, which in turn reveal something about the rocks, soil and climate. All around, the scents, colours and sounds are marking the moment precisely, while our experience is shaped by what we had for breakfast and what we got up to the night before. A furry creature becomes a key to unlocking everything around you and inside you.

We emerged from a habitat and we will return to a habitat, as mulch of some kind. Our experience in the short time between these two moments will be in some part determined by the interest we take in our habitat. It is hard to lead a poorer life by noticing more.

We are where we are because we have been drawn here by a conspiracy. It is a grand and wonderful conspiracy, one that snares every plant, animal and human being. It is so much more fun being snared voluntarily by a system we understand and enjoy than by one that baffles us.

In the following chapters we will step from looking at the broad connections that are easy for all to spot, towards some of the more extraordinary ones. The aim is to reach the point where the networks that these connections form touch the world that fascinates you. I have no idea exactly where that will be, but I am certain that if you have a heart pumping blood to your nervous system, it can be found.

III. Finding a Path

1. A Practical Way In

'Life is "trying things to see if they work".'
(RAY BRADBURY)

There is a popular saying amongst survivalists that we can last three minutes without air, three hours without warmth, three days without water and three weeks without food. This is looking up from the very bottom of Maslow's Pyramid of Needs and a great place to start. By the time we are half way up the psychologist's mini-mountain, we will have touched on our need for air, heat, water, food, navigation skills and medicine. But we shall not rest on the necessary, for there is much important, *un*necessary fun to be had, with a pencil and curious grimace to hand.

The expression 'a breath of fresh air' has become a worn metaphor, but like all clichés there is a shiny little nugget of truth concealed under its rust. Anyone who has ever tried meditation will know that there is breathing . . . and then there is *breathing*. Whole books have been written about breathing techniques, and diverse groups of people, from actors to archers, treat it as an art form.

This chapter is about doing things differently, because this will help us to sense and think differently. It is important that we overcome the inertia that likes to sidle up next to a reader. There is no need to do the exercises mentioned in this chapter as you read them, but the ideas in this book will not be able to tiptoe around your healthy scepticism if you do not at least attempt a few of them at some time. With that in mind, here is the first exercise.

Exercise 1

Whilst still indoors, I would like you to close your eyes (after reading the rest of this paragraph) and breathe ten times, deeply and slowly, in through your nostrils and out through your nostrils. If you have a heavy cold then the survivalists saying that we can live for three minutes without air will start to make perfect sense, but otherwise you should find this straightforward, if not particularly dramatic.

Now stand outdoors and repeat the exercise. Ten breaths, deeply, slowly, nostrils only.

Compare the experiences.

I cannot tell you how your two experiences will compare exactly, but I can be certain that there were differences. No two habitats are identical and this simple exercise goes some small way to proving it.

If you found it difficult or impossible to complete this task, then you are a very busy person. More specifically, your mind is very busy convincing you that you are so very busy that breathing is not an important exercise. Your mind is racing so hard and fast towards the promised land of achievement at the top of Maslow's pyramid that it has become convinced that there really is no time to contemplate breathing. The base has crumbled and this is not a stable pyramid. If you suspect that this may be true for you, then it might be a good idea to try a different exercise first, which is to hold a pillow over your face for a couple of minutes or until the importance of breathing becomes clear again, whichever comes first. That is a joke. Don't do that. Emphatically do not do that if you are an asthmatic solicitor.

It's tough-love time. Has it ever occurred to you that one of your ancient ancestors, the one with a balding back and a philosophy of violence that would make the Vikings blush, might actually have been better at breathing than you?

Feeling Secure

Enough with the breathing already. With oxygen coursing to our minds on the back of haemoglobin stallions, the next most pressing issue is our security. It is all very well being good at sucking in oxygen, but this is a wasted talent if our life story reads: they inhaled, they exhaled, they were gobbled up by a Bengal tiger. If you would like to counter at this point that Bengal tigers are rare beasts in Bengal and no less rare in Hemel Hempstead, then you have wandered into a trap. Mine.

However strong or weak our natural-history knowledge, there is a likelihood that we all retain a solid understanding of the big beasts in our home environments and the likelihood of encountering them.

Exercise 2

Have a look down the following checklist and tick the creatures you are likely to see in the next couple of months:

- Lion
- Panther

- Jaguar
- Elk
- Cow
- Sheep

Most people will find this exercise easy. That is the point: our awareness of our surroundings and our understanding of nature are already heavily influenced by our need for security.

You are reading this partly because your genes survived and empowered you with an automatic sensitivity to imminent threats in the animal kingdom. An awareness of the animals that can endanger us is part of being human. This is why we are so sensitive to motion – your brain will focus your attention on anything that moves before allowing you to take in stillness. A common rabbit will still make you look; only once you have identified it as neither threat nor opportunity will your brain allow your gaze to return to the magnificent colours of the maple leaf.

Those creatures that combine threat and elusiveness earn their own special place in our psyches, and they earned this reputation a lot earlier in our development than we can trace. Chimpanzees have a strong aversion to snakes, which can be seen in their physical reactions to them. The human wariness towards snakes is similarly strong and primal and, like all such fundamental emotions, we find it woven into stories, myths and legends. Adam and Eve were not tempted by a lamb.

Have you noticed that all children, however much they yearn for the squeaks and bleeps of computer games, can identify a stinging nettle? A child who fails to show any interest in a natural-history

Can you identify this plant?

museum will have a lively interest in a wasp that lands on their nose. Clear and present danger, or the perception of it, does a wonderful job of holding our attention. As I plant the thought that you may possibly have left something on – was it the oven, the iron? Or maybe it was something to do with a door lock . . . I'm just not sure – it is so much harder to concentrate. Where was I? Oh yes, security.

Security is not just about keeping ourselves out of the jaws of predators. In November 2011, David Austin, a 28-year-old from Derby, walked into a remote area of the Scottish Highlands with a plan to live rough off the land. His body was found in a bothy a few weeks later by a local worker. It wasn't for want of air, food or water that he perished. Sadly, David lost a battle with hypothermia.

Considering the dangers of exposure leads us to make a chain of connections with nature. It starts with the simple but life-saving realization that if we are too exposed we get very uncomfortable. The next time you go for a windy walk with a group of friends, notice how the underdressed one will migrate to be at the downwind edge of the group. If there is more than one cold person, then the group will subconsciously shuffle round each other like the emperor penguins do in Antarctica each winter. And this chilled sensation has led to a very practical bond with nature, in the form of our ancestors' use of animal fur to keep warm, a habit that only ebbed away recently to be replaced by more palatable options. (We now wear shirts made from Egyptian cotton instead. As is so often the case, when we feel shame at our use of natural resources, we change the part of nature we turn to for help, but we can never turn our backs entirely.)

Spend enough time with outdoors people and you will hear the following saying: 'There is no such thing as bad weather, only inappropriate clothing.' But when we insulate ourselves against the elements, we inevitably insulate ourselves from the need for awareness also. If you do find yourself as the underdressed one, there will be some compensation in the fact you are probably also the one with the most intense experience of your environment, however uncomfortable that may be. You will find yourself acutely aware of which direction the wind is coming from and perhaps the shape and shade of the clouds in that direction.

Fortunately, there is no need to march out into a wilderness dressed only in shorts, vest and a crazy smile to achieve this raised awareness. It is a better idea to dress well and pay active attention, as opposed to the passive kind ushered on by feeling too cold.

The difference between active and passive attention is worth thinking about. Indoors, we might take a second to think about the unusual scent in the air. If we do, we might pick up that strangely familiar whiff of dust on hot metal and then make the fair conclusion that the oven is still on. This is not the same as leaving it on overnight, then leaning back during breakfast the following morning and burning an elbow. I have done both, so I know that the first felt better to both my mind and my elbow. Outdoors, the potential for moving from the latter approach to the former is everywhere.

Reading the Sky

By tuning into what our eyes, ears, nose and face are trying to tell us about the sky, we open up half of a new world. The wind direction, its temperature and the scents it brings with it are all easy to read and we can do this without running the risk of hypothermia. We can actually go much further, by reminding ourselves of skills that have been waning for centuries, but which are now enjoying a small revival.

Looking back in history, we see a steady regression from triple-glazing, Gore-tex boots and thermal mid-layers to a much thinner barrier between us and nature. Draughty stone houses without glass were once the best shelter there was, and before that many homes were made from turf and turd-bound straw. It is no wonder that in earlier times we find a sharp curiosity and keen ability to read the sky itself. The sky formed half of an ancient's experience of the world, whereas the modern traveller sees it as a fluctuating superficial layer at best. The last vestiges of this awareness and knowledge can be found in 'weather lore', the collection of sayings used to help us forecast and prepare.

Many have heard the most popular of these sayings, 'Red sky at night, shepherd's delight', but far fewer know from experience or theory whether it holds any stock. It does. If the sky is red at the end of the day, then it follows that the visibility is good in the west, which is the direction the weather is usually coming from in the northern hemisphere; the outlook is therefore good. There are hundreds of these nuggets that sit just out of popular reach or memory. They can form a fun and practical new way of connecting with half of the outdoors world.

The best time to get started in this area is following a spell of good weather: it is much easier to predict a deterioration than an improvement. This is not least because you can see a lot more detail in the sky on a sunny day, than squinting up through low, drizzle-bearing grey rugs.

Almost every traditional culture has woven somewhere within its folklore a version of the idea that good weather will turn bad when high wispy clouds appear and then a thin mist appears in front of the sun, moon or stars. This thin layer of high misty cloud is called cirrostratus, and it can cause light to refract and form a circle around the sun and moon. The Zuni Indians of North America used to interpret this halo as a tepee: the sun was going into its tepee for shelter as rain was on its way.

One western version is nicely encapsulated with this piece of lore: 'Mare's tails and mackerel scales make tall ships bring in their sails.' The wispy, candy-floss-like clouds that form 'mare's tails' are called cirrus. When a blue sky is visited by cirrus followed by cirrostratus, there is a high probability that these are the clouds at the leading edge of a warm front. Warm fronts bring lots of rain.

Exercise 3

During the next spell of fine weather, pay close attention to the blue sky a few times each day. Look for high candy-floss wisps of cirrus and also for high misty cirrostratus that will show up most clearly to the side of the sun and stars, occasionally forming a halo. (Never look directly at the sun.)

Note how bad weather never arrives without a few warning signs. Sunny days do not metamorphose into rainy ones with a flick of a switch, but with a progression of clouds and wind changes, and this progression is easy to spot.

When new to these techniques it is best to cheat a bit and look at dependable local forecasts to see when the good weather is due to break. As you get closer to this time, you can concentrate your

Mares' tails – rain may be on its way.

search. With practice it becomes possible to forecast the change independently and without official forecasts. Sometimes it is even possible to predict changes that the professionals have failed to forecast, using techniques that predate the meteorologists' supercomputers by thousands of years. This will give you a sense of accomplishment quite unlike the gratification that comes from more artificial rewards, like earning money or buying something, whether you try it on a windswept hill or outside a shopping mall.

After the Sun Has Set

Having kept hypothermia at bay using forecasting rhymes that make you sound like a mad old moor-dweller, I suggest you spend a night in the wild. Metaphorically.

Good clothing, whether fake fur or silk thermals, and a sensitivity to the elements will keep you warm and comfortable for a full day, but if you stop moving at night then the experience of exposure changes too. Shelter is necessary if you are planning on spending any serious time outdoors at night. The skills to provide this are something that we seem to be programmed to accumulate.

Imagine for a second you are on a long walk with an outdoors expert and you find yourself in a situation where you need to spend the night outdoors unexpectedly. You have no tent or other options on your back. All you have is a knife. If the outdoors-person turns to you and says 'Let's build a shelter,' you may initially think that you lack the necessary skills to do a good job. However, if they phrase it slightly differently, 'Let's make a camp,' there is a much higher chance that those early childhood experiences of mucking about with everything from cushions to tree branches will come flooding back. Most people get through life without needing to make a shelter in earnest, but few make it to adulthood without having made a camp of some sort.

The need for shelter has led humans to develop a strong connection with the plants that can help with shelter and warmth. Pines have been treasured for their usefulness in building homes like log cabins.

Once the dwelling has been built, the tired new owner may put their feet up, sitting on furniture made from locally coppiced beech. They will then warm their toes on a charcoal fire using fuel from the same coppice.

One of the fastest ways to feel a connection with nature and our ancestors is to light a fire using the best natural materials as the tinder. Old man's beard, also known as traveller's joy or *Clematis vitalba*, is the fluffy white climbing plant you will have seen adorning hedgerows in late summer. Try gathering some and using it as the tinder to get a fire started. (Those with a penchant for health and safety must choose their spot especially carefully, avoiding starting forest fires, house fires or setting themselves on fire.)

There is no need to go the whole way and make a bow-drill, an ancient fire-lighting tool; a match can be used to ignite the tinder. It is the chain of events leading from simple actions that is important. You are warmed by a fire that actually lit because your knowledge of your environment allowed you to source an effective tinder, instead of resorting to reeking firelighters or the familiar and depressing action of flicking matches endlessly into a pile of damp leaves and twigs that fail to catch. I can guarantee that you will never look at the determined but humble clematis the same way again. It will refuse to blend into the background of the hedge, emerging instead to remind you of your warm friendship.

Meeting Water in Different Circumstances

Thirst will pick its moment to totally change the way you see the world. Most months I travel from a cosseted home environment, where I turn my nose up at a glass of water that has some harmless speck swirling at the bottom, to drinking water from a flask that is cleverly tinted to make the swirly things invisible.

Many years ago, as a teenager, I found myself lost on the slopes of an Indonesian volcano. At the end of the second hot day with no food and little water, I lowered a clear plastic flask into a shallow stagnant puddle, lifted the half-full canister up to the light and watched the minute critters fidgeting and bouncing up from the sediment at the bottom. They twitched and writhed. Then I added the sterilizing tablet, waited until the twitching stopped, waited some more and drank it eagerly, leaving a little at the bottom for good measure. There are tales of travellers who have tried to drink the fuel in their stoves and Bedouin who kill camels to drink their blood and stomach contents, such is the power of thirst.

Anyone who has been desperately thirsty in the wilderness will take an interest in any water that is passed. Serious thirst turns all travellers who have experienced it into prospectors, never far from the frenzy of excitement that a good find brings. From majestic cataracts to pathetic puddles, the thought is there: it is water and can be drunk. But what sort of elixir would it prove? One that tickled the throat and then happily became one with our every organ? Or one that resisted swallowing and then made for the exits?

Stop by the next stagnant water you see. Peer in. Lower your cupped hands into the murk and lift it close to your lips. Sniff it. Imagine it sliding down your throat . . . Now drop it and remember to wash your hands. Do this a couple of times and you will never look at a puddle the same way again. For better or worse.

The practical rule for water is to do your best to check the safety of the source and avoid the stagnant stuff altogether, if possible. Spring water is safest, but in all cases boiling does the best job of reducing the need for toilet paper in the subsequent hours.

Foraging for More than Food

The great renaissance is well underway in the world of foraging. Restaurants that don't claim to have mushrooms that have been hand-picked from within a couple of miles are not taken seriously any more, and are far from the vanguard of this movement. True and scary scarcity led to the government encouraging all to reap the 'hedgerow harvest' during the Second World War. The baton was picked up in the UK by Richard Mabey with his book *Food for Free* in the 1970s. And then more recently it has been carried with such élan by practitioners like Miles Irving that the suspicion must be that there are performance-enhancing fungi out there.

It's true of foragers, as it is of practitioners of other ancient, fundamental skills, that our instinct is often to patronize them. Isn't it so . . . lovely, so quaint? A nice mug of nettle soup to enjoy as you wash the berry stains from toes that poke out of sandals. Elderflower fritter, anyone? It is all so adorable! (With inevitable suspicions of 'alternative' personal hygiene.)

Even amongst foraging's supporters, this is a broad and entrenched attitude and hard to overturn. I think that Miles Irving does a very good job of taking an unemotional axe to it with this fact: people were up to 15cm taller before agriculture, because 10,000 years ago their diet contained up to five times more plant types.

Foraging offers a deep, rich and fascinating world for those who choose to pursue it keenly. It also offers very easy entry points for those who wish to dabble. The fastest way to nurture a connection with nature through foraging is to seek out something you have never eaten before and swallow it – having taken the small but important precaution of checking that it is not poisonous.

If we look at some of the most accessible wild foods – elder-flowers and -berries, blackberries, nettles, dandelions – there is a good chance that you have sampled one or more but not all. Or perhaps you have tried many of them, but not from your own fair hand. Pick one, literally, that you have not sought out before, cook it and delight yourself by proving how eating it does not lead to a slow and painful death. There comes a moment for many who are totally new to foraging when they make a startling discovery: not only does wild food not lead automatically to hospital, but it can actually go some way towards taking away feelings of hunger.

There comes a moment when these basic activities allow us to meet our ancestors briefly. Glancing past some nettles, we catch a glimpse of their hairy faces smiling back at us, and grunting something to the effect of 'We might have been savages, but we weren't idiots,' before they slope off to settle a mild dispute by clubbing someone to death. Fortunately, we can enjoy the best of both worlds: it is possible to revel in the satisfaction of fundamental activities, without the need to witness blunt trauma.

Foraging, like all outdoor skills, initially shows us the natural world through a very basic lens. Plants are either poisonous, edible or of little interest. As the skill develops the lens becomes refined. We learn to associate certain plants with certain times of the year, and to cherish those that offer us nutrition when the ground is barest. A new respect is found for plants that shrug off winter, like the dandelion; the season widens our gaze, leading us to discover roots underground.

Experts in most arts find the greatest joy in the subtleties, paradoxes and challenges of their art. Black bryony has edible young shoots but poisonous berries. The more we get to know each part of the natural world, the more we realize that while it is tempting to pigeonhole simplistically, it is not always realistic. This is true of most plants, animals and people we encounter.

In truth, foraging on its own is a lean business. It can stave off hunger for a period, especially in late summer, but suffice it to say that foragers are not the target of recent campaigns to stem the obesity epidemic. It takes higher-energy foodstuffs to build reserves, and such foodstuffs have plans of their own. The art of making a plan that is smarter than the plan of the food you are trying to eat is called 'hunting'.

An Impossible Attempt at a Dispassionate Look at Hunting

Hunting is not for everyone and is misunderstood by almost everyone. If we include fishing, then the outdoor pursuit of animals is one of the most popular activities in the world, for both survival and pleasure. I am not a hunter or fisherman. I find no pleasure in killing anything – but that is also true of a surprising number of hunters and fishermen. Without writing a dedicated and much longer book than this one, it is hard to tackle the difference between mindless murder and hunting in a way that will not irritate everyone and alienate both groups. I can sympathize with both camps and am delighted that it is a source of passionate debate. So long as somebody is passionate about an outdoor issue, then they are a naturalist of some kind, and in a better position than somebody who goes their whole life thinking green is little more than an unlikely choice of car colour.

It is, however, interesting to note the number of hunters who maintain the urge to follow the every movement of their prey, but find the final kill harder with passing years. I know ex-members of the SAS who hunt occasionally, but who have found killing animals gets harder over time. Their names are safe with me. If an enthusiasm for the kill wanes, that does not mean a desire to understand and predict your prey's movements will also decline. Often it is the camera that replaces the lethal weapon. Whatever someone carries in their hand as they crawl through the undergrowth, they have their connection, and that small fact is beyond debate.

Tracks of Land and Sky

One of the many arts born from hunting has become an independent subject of its own: tracking. A shallow impression in long-dried mud that goes unnoticed by most who walk past will suddenly whisper questions up at the individual who develops an interest in tracking. Who, what, when and why? A couple of bland tracks become a short story when we identify them as those of a dog chasing a deer.

If we follow them along the path and through a break in the dense undergrowth, an excited heartbeat pushes us up a hill to a clearing. Then a few more twists and turns and the tracks disappear. We catch a breath and look around. Our feet no longer drum below, but the silence is temporary: a pigeon rustles the leaves overhead. Thoughts of the creatures we were tracking have flown away too, and instead we see our ancestor friend sat on a log, sharpening a stick:

'You're lost, aren't you?'

'Yes.'

'How can you be lost? The moon is there.'

Someone who has never felt lost is probably going to reach an unpleasant place in time, the one where they realize that they regret the things they didn't do a lot more than the ones they did. Getting lost and then finding our way back is part of a life that balances an abundance of fresh discovery with an avoidance of premature death.

After many years of using compasses, maps, charts and then increasingly screens and dials, I realized that humanity had increased the accuracy of navigation at the expense of romance. Within a few seconds of discovering that it was possible to navigate using the sun, moon, stars, weather, plants and animals, I knew that the natural world had me in its sights. That is one of nature's best tricks. We don't start by finding nature itself interesting – it is almost meaningless in its vagueness – but we will all at some point discover the part of nature that corresponds with our own inner passions, whatever they might be. My interest in natural navigation crept up on me stealthily at first, but then took over my life. There are many interests that spring up and last for a shorter time.

We will all develop a sudden interest in natural medicine if it promises a cure for a problem that is otherwise hard to tackle. The same children who recognize a stinging nettle so easily because of its painful effects learn their first natural medicine in the form of the dock leaf that can be rubbed on stings to make them less painful. Dock leaves do contain an antihistamine which may help soothe the sting, but the efficacy of this is still debated by scientists. The same scientists who are happy to refute the value of a dock leaf indoors are probably as likely as any of us to reach for one when stung outdoors. That is the difference between empirical knowledge and painful ankles.

Since the part of the spectrum of life we find interesting changes as we grow older, so do the portals which will draw us towards nature. We move from an interest in risk and upheaval to a fondness for familiarity and security. An eight-year-old will be happy to learn about yew trees if you couch their story in the context of bow-and-arrow making. Forty years later, the same person will tend to find gardening a more dependable entry point than archery, but the principle is identical.

Exercises 4 and 5

Notice how the sun is due south in the middle of the day. This is true every day of the year, from everywhere north of the Tropic of Cancer, i.e. all of Europe and the US.

The next time you see a crescent moon high in the sky, join the horns of the moon in a straight line and extend this line down to your horizon. You will be looking roughly south.

The crescent moon can give a quick, rough guide to south.

Now turn to your savage friend and take him down a peg. Explain that TV satellite dishes can be use to navigate: in the UK they tend to point close to southeast.

Creating Awareness

Creative types do not like to believe that they will find much of interest by grazing down at the bottom of Maslow's pyramid. Thinking about food and shelter is all too mundane, practical, nuts-and-boltsy for artists and writers. These creatures see themselves as the giraffes, grazing from the higher levels, the top branches of creativity and self-actualization. Fortunately there are plenty of those. Bark-rubbing and leaf-pressing may be too childish for some tastes, but the simplest exercises are often the best.

A person who sketches a tree, regardless of their artistic ability, will see a tree in a way that is almost impossible otherwise. Go for it. What have you got to lose, but your dreams of erecting a soiled tent in the Tate Modern?

Anyone who has ever wanted or needed to write about nature ends up with a notebook of some kind. Once you start to write about something, you observe it in more detail than can possibly be remembered. With the slightest encouragement, our senses run riot and bombard our less-than-match-fit minds with such a wealth of detail that we need help storing it.

Exercises 6 and 7

Spend ten minutes sketching a tree.

Now write a short story about the experience of looking at a tree in this way. If you find conflict in your scene, brilliant, use it. If not, search for it. It can be the sight of past violence: trauma done to the tree by animals or insects, lightning, snapping, or the decay and death of a branch. Or it can be an inner conflict: perhaps the effort required to complete this exercise makes you angry or reminds you of an English teacher you disliked. If you still have no luck, invent it . . . You never know, you might enjoy it.

The End Game

For a few, none of the exercises in this chapter so far will trigger a deep response. This is not the end of the road for them, but the start of a game. Games offer a cunning way of teaching new ideas to those who find advice difficult and structure reassuring. (Have you ever tried suggesting a small rule-change to an aficionado of Monopoly halfway through a game? Of course not. It would be less stressful to build a real hotel.)

Games allow us to look at one small part of life in controlled conditions. Like a good illusionist, they make us look at the things we did not expect to see. Nature games are no different. If someone tells us to go and smell the woodland floor, we will likely resist. But a good game of hide-and-seek will give us all a lifelong love of the smell of rotting leaves.

Joseph Cornell was a pioneer of games that help children to connect with nature. He noticed that when he toured internationally and presented these games to groups from all over the world, he received the same reaction:

'These games are very Japanese,' the Japanese told him.

'These games are very Greek,' the Greeks assured him.

They were of course the same games. We know we are near universal truths when other nationalities can find no difference with us. National disagreements may stretch all the way down from nuclear weapons to cheese-making, but they do appear to stop at nature games.

Exercise 8

My favourite natural navigation game is to get one person to lead a group on a walk none of them know. Crucially, everyone other than the leader is denied reference to maps, compasses or GPS. When we have reached the pub for lunch, each person in the group must sketch out the route we took on a piece of paper. Like many games it sounds simple – and is, on one level. But try it for yourself one day and I promise that *doing* this simple thing will make you look at the world in a fresh way.

Once you have used a tree to help find your way, your relationship with it changes. It stands out and its relationship with the sun, wind and your path become more apparent.

2. The Senses

'What is called our experience is almost entirely
determined by our habits of attention.'
(WILLIAM JAMES)

In December 2004 the Jarawa tribe headed away from the coast, where they liked to hunt turtles, and up into the hill country of the Andaman Islands. Then the biggest wave imaginable hit the shore.

The Jarawa had managed to sense and escape the Asian tsunami that destroyed the ground and life where they had been standing. They were tuned to the clues of imminent upheaval in the land, sea and animals around them, and this instinctive sensory awareness saved their lives. The cry of birds and the way marine animals' behaviour changed shortly before the tsunami gave the indigenous people just enough warning to escape to higher ground.

The Jarawa saved their lives, but this chapter is about the way the senses that help preserve our lives can also enhance our lives. There is a gulf between being alive and dead, but this gulf is not the same size for everybody. John Burroughs, an American writer and naturalist in the late nineteenth century, was ahead of the game when he wrote, 'There is nothing people differ in more than in their powers of observation. Some are only half alive.'

Nobody wakes up in the morning and decides to shut down their senses and stumble through each day in an oblivious bubble, and yet some people end up having much richer experiences than others. If two people go for an identical walk, one of them might have a profounder, more fascinating experience than the other, but why? One reason will be each person's life experiences to date.

A study by the US military found that soldiers of equal military experience did not see the world in the same way. Most critically, some soldiers were markedly better at spotting potential dangers, like improvised explosive devices and other ambushes. The two groups that stood out in this research were those with a hunting background and those who came from tough urban neighbourhoods. These groups had clearly been conditioned by their former experiences to see the world as a mixture of threats and opportunities: a lack of awareness translated into a bad day of different sorts to each group, and, as a consequence, their senses were finely tuned to any anomalies in their landscape.

We are unlikely to want to enlist the help of insurgents or urban thugs to sharpen our senses, and any attempt to hone our senses through the introduction of fear will only appeal to a minority. It is true that those who jump off tall buildings with parachutes develop a forensic level of understanding of the elements, but those who make mistakes also experience a marked deterioration in their sensual ability when they hit the concrete below at 150 miles per hour. There are better ways to enrich our experience of life.

There is enough evidence of people experiencing the world in transformative ways to make us believe it is both possible and achievable. The improvements we can enjoy from time spent in nature are physical and physiological – we become fitter, happier and learn to use our senses more effectively – but they are also philosophical. One of the early pioneers of our modern reconnection with nature, Henry David Thoreau, wrote that 'two or three hours' walking will carry me to as strange a country as I expect ever to see.'

If we notice ten times as much when we step outside, then one mile will feel like a ten-mile walk used to (to our minds, that is, but mercifully not our legs).

If we wish to notice more, it is a good idea to slow down; and noticing more will itself tend to make you slow down. This is true whatever you focus on. My fascination with natural navigation means I am pulled back by wildflowers, clouds, trees, rocks, planets and even puddles. Paths that I could have bounded along as an ignorant teenager have become treacle, as my senses arrest my progress. I now find it much harder to go for the really long walks I used to, not because I have lost the ability physically, but because I notice so much now that I am repeatedly confronted with the same awkward and unwelcome decision: take too long or ignore things? It takes a certain immaturity to walk over twenty miles in one day and not feel your head overload with sensual input. I know.

How many senses are there? Five? Six? Some say between ten and thirty. Proprioception is the sense we have of where our joints are, even though we can't see them: we can tell where our hands are when our eyes are closed. We have all sensed thirst, hunger, tiredness, low blood-sugar . . . It is easy to see how the list grows, but the philosophy for each is identical and so we can focus on the ones we know best, and the lessons from these can be applied elsewhere if we choose.

Sight

The sense of sight is the best one to start working with as it is the most familiar and powerful for most people. But this power comes at a cost: our sight is so effective at getting the basics done that we lazily overlook its full potential.

Our eyes pass so much detailed information to our brain that our brain has been forced to develop coping and filtering strategies. Inevitably we fail to notice most of what we see, because we can only concentrate on a portion of the canvas presented to us. This has been demonstrated with a smile in the 'gorilla basketball experiment', where an audience is shown a clip of two people passing a basketball to each other and asked to count the number of passes. In the background a man dressed as a gorilla enters the court and wanders about. Asked if they saw anything unusual on the court, the audience fails to come up with anything. The audience all laugh at their partial blindness when they are told to watch the clip again and look for the gorilla, not count the passes. In another very amusing example of our imperfect visual attention, a film is shown of an actor stopping to ask a stranger for directions. As they chat, a large wooden door is carried between them. In the brief moment that they cannot see each other, the actor ducks away and swaps with someone else. As the door is carried away and the view is no longer blocked, the stranger continues the conversation, entirely oblivious to the fact they have metamorphosed into a different human being. Both great fun, but what value for those with an interest in nature?

Exercise 9

PART I

Go for a three-minute walk outdoors. Note down the things your eyes are drawn towards.

If we have an understanding of the things our brain is likely to prioritize then we can temporarily override this pecking order and we will start to see new things.

PART II

Repeat your three-minute walk, following the same route, only this time try to ignore anything that moves, as much as is safely possible. Let your eyes be drawn to things that remain still. Ignore everything that shows any motion at all, people, animals, leaves in a breeze. It should feel a little peculiar and lead to you noticing at least a few things that you overlooked on your first walk.

Our brains have learned to notice things that move, so if we make a special effort to look for things that are still we see a subtly different world. I would ask you to repeat your walk, this time looking for things with shapes and colours you find the most boring – but asking you to do so might test your enthusiasm for this exercise, so it can be a theoretical walk for now. We have survived as examples of our species because we successfully prioritize the things that are likely to be a threat or an opportunity. It is harder to get killed by things that are still, or boring colours, as this eliminates most predators and a lot of poisons.

We all see the world through a prism, our own personal lens, one that is shaped by both our experience and our goals. My work means that I spend a lot of time outdoors with experts and specialists – geographers, geologists, botanists, farmers, soldiers, artists, foragers, foresters – and one of the things I have found most interesting is that we are all incapable of experiencing the same patch of earth in the same way. We are all conditioned to look for certain things in certain places.

There is one particular experiment I like to conduct on my natural navigation courses that demonstrates the challenges and opportunities available by understanding our own personal lens. Early in one of my outdoors courses, I lead people up a short, steep, muddy bank of a field and then show them a tree, next to a fence, in the middle distance. I give them the following instructions: 'I'd like you to stare at this tree for a whole minute. I want you to burn an image of its silhouette into your retina. Try to learn and memorize its shape and outline. Once you have done this we are going to walk for one minute and during this time it is very important that you don't look back at the tree.'

I'd like you to look at the photograph on this page, it is the view that my students get and I'd like you to stare at the tree too.

Study this tree shape for 1 minute before reading on.

My students and I then walk for a minute, during which I make sure they do not peek at the tree. When we have reached the right spot, I ask them to turn round and look at the tree they think they know so well. Now look at the second photograph below.

Southwest is to the left of the picture; this is the direction the wind has come from.

The single tree has become two trees and completely changed shape. Most students are pleasantly shocked to have seen me wield my powers of magic in this way: 'What pact has he made with the dark forces?' is a line I hear them say to each other quite regularly. (That's not true, but the rest is.)

I go on to explain that we can notice that certain trees are windswept and this can tell us where southwest is, since this is the direction that the prevailing winds blow from in the UK. My second point – which is more important than the simple technique of direction-finding – is that a tree's appearance changes each time we look at it from a new spot; a tree gradually metamorphoses as we take each step. So far, so simple, but on more than one occasion this lesson did not go exactly as I had expected.

The aim of these courses is for me to help people see the world through a different lens to the one they are used to – a very specific natural navigation lens. The walks allow me to show students some of the things that practised observation can reveal in this one discipline, and the best places to look for them. The embarrassing truth is that during the visual experiment above, in the very short walk from one perspective point to another, which I know very well, I have had my own partial vision demonstrated to me. On various occasions, I have had an orchid, a fossilized animal and a bird of prey – a red kite – pointed out to me by other specialists. All these things I had failed to pick out through my lens of the moment. There were certainly innumerable other things that everyone in each group overlooked.

What is the broader lesson? I think that a focused interest is a two-edged sword: it allows us to notice many things that pass others by, but it narrows the spotlight of our vision. A keen passion for one area of nature will definitely encourage you to spot many things, but not everything. To use both edges of this sword in a positive way, we need to develop our interests, but then remain conscious of the blind spots these might introduce.

Natural navigation has made me weak at noticing some insects, but I am usually the first in a group to spot a planet at dusk. A forager will spot the ripening red on a bush before the tracker, but the tracker will notice the tiny thread of fur hanging off a thorn next to it. Staring into the distance, a sailor will notice the coming wind-change painted in the clouds, as the soldier spots the glint reflected off binoculars on the hill below them.

Experience will also teach us how the world appears differently with changes in light and the angle of the sun. Sailors learn to look 'down-sun' (with the sun behind you) when searching for something at sea, otherwise the glare blots everything out, but to look 'up-moon' as this is the best way to pick out detail in the low moonlight. Trackers like to look at details on the ground 'up-sun' as this casts more helpful shadows. Natural navigators know that you get the shortest shadows from a stick in the middle of the day, when the sun is highest, and that these cast a perfect north–south shadow line.

In time, everybody learns their own way to read the shift in shade, shadow and colour as the day and year progress. We can all appreciate the way flowers appear differently in the diffuse light of a spring morning than they do in the more intense sunlight of midday in summer.

It is a very rewarding exercise to do the same walk repeatedly, but with a different focus each time. (I sometimes like to put a different book in my backpack on each walk. Very often I don't get it out at all, it just sits there and silently reminds me of the area I'm trying to focus on.) Then, allow a little time to pass and return to the walk without a specific focus or aim, but to enjoy a richer experience than you had on any one occasion previously.

Hearing

Before we analyse our sense of hearing it is worth doing another quick exercise.

Exercise 10

Stand outside and listen for one minute. Note down everything you hear.

Our sense of hearing is considered the weaker sense, but it has one very big advantage over sight: it is far less focused directionally. You can hear something that you cannot see – something behind your head, for example. Every moment outdoors is an opportunity to build an aural landscape, and it is possible to do this without consciously searching for anything.

An interest in what your ears are trying to describe for you will lead you to many discoveries that would otherwise go unnoticed, and this art of listening is likely to follow a progression:

1. We notice certain sounds and listen attentively to them for the first time.

2. We build a picture of the constant sounds, the fluctuating sounds and the intermittent sounds.

3. We identify the sounds.

4. We build a relationship between our location and these sounds.

5. We mentally map the territory through sound.

6. We learn how the map changes with time.

Listening for one minute, we might notice the following sounds: birdsong, the low rumble of a distant motorway, the wind in the trees. Each of these sounds is trying to enrich our understanding of our location. There is information about time of day, time of year, local animals, present and future weather, navigation clues and human behaviour.

As with what we see, each person's experience and focus will lead them to create a different picture. The birdwatcher may make the following assessment: 'There is a lot of birdsong, which I would expect at this time of day and year. I can hear the song of two distant male chiffchaffs. That means I must be standing close to the border of each male's territory. I am standing at the Checkpoint Charlie for chiffchaffs. This means that whichever way I walk I will move into one of their territories and away from the other's.'

The barefoot weather forecaster may note: 'I can hear the wind rustling the trees to the northeast. A wind blowing from the northeast is not typical; the prevailing direction in the UK is from the southwest. This means that, although it is settled at the moment, I can expect unusual weather and a likely drop in temperature very soon, as cold air from over the continent reaches us.'

During some courses I like to lead people through dense woodland twice, once before an eyes-closed listening exercise and once after it. In the first patch of woodland, I ask everyone to close their eyes and spin themselves round, up to the point where they are totally disorientated, but still standing up. Then, with their eyes still shut, I ask them to point north. Few succeed. I have ensured that there is no bright sunlight, detectable breeze, land gradient or other non-visual clues to help them. There is one clue, but few tune into it without being prompted. The natural navigator needs to note similar things to both the birder and the forecaster, but also make a mental note of the direction of man-made noises – in this case, the motorway.

On the second walk through woodland, after making sure that everyone has noted that the dull distant murmur of the motorway is to the north, everyone can point north with their eyes closed effortlessly.

Listening attentively is a habit that is transferable into new areas. For example, if you listen carefully for a few weeks at home, you might start to become familiar with the bark of your neighbour's dog. It might be possible to refine the art, so that you can distinguish between the bark that means another animal is passing by, and the bark that means that it is dinner time. You might even be able to distinguish between the bark that means a *person* is passing and one that means a person with a dog on a lead is passing.

Once you start listening in this way, you make many fresh discoveries and find new heroes. There are blind people who can describe a street by listening to the echoes of the clicks they make with their tongue. I love the way bakers pull a sponge from the oven and then lower an ear to the browning surface of the mixture to listen for gas escaping, or the old-timer mechanics who can identify the spark-plug that needs changing by cocking one ear.

One consequence of listening carefully is that we tend to become more aware of the creatures that can hear us too, including other people. If you are keeping a 'listening watch', you will notice the approach of other people before they become aware of your presence. This becomes a matter of pride for some.

You will also notice how silence reduces the likelihood of animals scarpering before you hear them, and therefore improves your chances of detecting them. The number of deer you see on a group walk will be inversely proportional to the number of people having a conversation. Squirrels in a wood, for example, tend to smell or hear us, then see us, then bound away across the forest floor to a tree-trunk escape. All we hear is the last rustle of leaves, like audible dust on our horizon. If you stay both still and silent, however, then the tables are often turned, especially in the case of upwind animals, and you get to see the creatures doing their work instead of hotfooting it. The American Indian technique of 'still-hunting', picking a spot and waiting silently for prey to find you, is just as effective when your intention is observation.

As our understanding of the way animals listen grows, we may ask ourselves the question: what do *plants* hear? Every year it seems there are more newspaper stories about the music plants prefer; there was even one recently about their favoured regional accent – Geordie, apparently. I hate to be the one to bang a loud cymbal and smash these notions, but there is no scientific evidence of plants reacting to music or noise of any kind. None. They are deaf. If that saddens you, then feel free to let your emotions go; the sound of your weeping will not slow the growth of the forest.

It is impossible to hear the same soundtrack twice outdoors. If we think we do, then it is just a sign that we are not focusing on what we hear. Our sensitivity to time is one measure of our sense of hearing. We will hear the minutes passing in the coming and going of creatures, the hours passing in the rise and fall of birdsong, and the months passing as every single sound shifts: the wind we hear in the trees changes as the leaves fall, and the sounds of our footsteps ebb with each fall of rain or snow.

The years pass and this is marked sadly by the fall in skylark song or, more cheerfully, by a new neighbourly owl.

Exercise 11

Stand outside, where you stood before, and listen for one minute. Note down everything you hear and the conclusions you are able to make. Forecast the weather, map the human and bird territories, point north with your eyes closed, but lack not ambition!

There were two people listening to nature today and they were both you, but one ought to be quietly impressed by the other.

Smell, Taste and Touch

Our nostrils contain clocks and calendars. I know this is true and if I forget it, then I will be reminded when, for instance, each nostril chimes together one June twilight with a honeysuckle waft. Our mouths struggle to keep up, but they can sometimes pick up the passing of the months in the sugars in the fruits. We taste the year passing in apples that roll from wincing sour to tongue-tickling sweet.

Our experience of smell and taste are intertwined and each is hardwired into an interesting part of our brains. These are the only two senses connected directly to our hippocampus, where our long-term memory resides. All other senses are routed via different parts and get processed elsewhere before finding their way to the hippocampus. A photograph of our schooldays will not whisk us back to that time as fast as the smell of cut grass and lawnmower exhaust or – worse, but faster still – the musty dank of the changing rooms.

Alongside the stinging nettle, we all quickly learn to recognize brambles. It is hard sometimes to persuade children to pause a moment to admire the colours of an early purple orchid, but when they have been snared and scratched by brambles a few times they are happy to conduct their own lessons in awareness: 'Watch out! Let's find another way.'

Fortunately when we are young we are resilient and have deep wells of enthusiasm to draw on. Our next lesson, after a bramble scratch, might be to trip over an inconspicuous root and feel that sore marker of youth: cold wet mud congealing on raw red palms. Our sense of touch begins with these painful reminders, but as our experience grows we use it to swerve around the most dramatic sensations and look for subtler triggers. We come to know that a teasel will tickle but not hurt and that each tree's bark feels different, from the aloof flat coolness of a beech to the warm corkiness of a field maple.

Human touch is one of the most intimate experiences. We are all aware of the rules of engagement regarding touch with other people. A hand placed on someone's shoulder is different to a hand on the waist and the potential for clear and mixed signals is well known. Animals in the wild rarely let us touch them, and plants seem oblivious; but we can be surprised by both. One of my fondest memories is of a tame squirrel, made fearless by the number of walkers that must have passed the same way, climbing up my leg and drinking from the water bottle that rested on my knee.

But what about these nonchalant plants? Any that react to our presence have the potential to intrigue. Experiments have shown that the majority of plants will react adversely to repetitive touching. Trees that are repeatedly buffeted by the wind will grow shorter and stouter trunks than sheltered ones, leading to wedge-shaped copses on hillsides. But like people, some plants are more sensitive than others. The burr cucumber is ten times more sensitive to touch than humans. Scientists have shown that these vines will grow towards the lightest of touches of a piece of string. This is biologically very impressive, but as animals we are unlikely to be bowled over by such slow reactions: it is *visible* movement that we react to most strongly.

The *Mimosa pudica* grows in the Americas and is both very sensitive to touch and willing to show it. If you touch the *Mimosa pudica*, its leaflets rapidly recoil, folding inwards and then drooping. The *pudica* part of the name is a clue – it means 'shy' in Latin. Its names in Hebrew and Bengali translate as 'don't touch me' and the 'shy virgin' respectively and respectably.

We can remind ourselves of the power of touch by closing our eyes again. The blind, as is so often the case, lead the way in this field. A Braille wristwatch has been developed that allows a blind person to tell the time with their fingers, but for many blind people these prove unnecessary as they are already able to tell the time with a broader sense of touch. By remaining sensitive to shifts in sunlight angles, temperatures and the atmosphere, these individuals have a sense of time that is more 'real' than numbers.

Trees that are repeatedly buffeted by the wind will grow shorter and stouter trunks than sheltered ones, leading to wedge-shaped copses on hillsides.

Exploring the senses means investigating a range of ideas, techniques and experiences. When new to any of these it is best to absorb and practise them in isolated ways. When we are comfortable with them individually, we can bring several together in one experience. The whole becomes greater than the sum of the parts.

Soon we experience the outdoors in a way that makes our earlier view of it seem a pale imitation. Edward O. Wilson described the higher awareness that it is possible to achieve as the 'naturalists' trance', whereby biologists are able to locate more elusive organisms. We can all use it to hunt the most elusive of creatures: the perfect nature experience.

3. The Big Relationships

*'Hirsute Highland heifers graze in fields greener
than guacamole.'*
(ALAN TAYLOR)

There is a lot of stuff out there. Mostly green stuff, with a few other
scattered colours and, at first, none of it seems to betray to the viewer
a lot of thought in the *way* it has been scattered.

If you have a space in your house where you chuck things that
have no other logical home – a big cupboard, an attic, an entire
garage – then you will know the feeling I am referring to here. The
one that comes from being confronted with a lot of stuff with no
apparent beauty, system, method, purpose or allure. This feeling of
mild dread sits close to the sensation of watching the contents of a
full bin-bag empty onto the floor through a tear in the bottom. It is
the feeling of being gently overwhelmed by chaos, and nobody likes
to be overwhelmed. (*Whelmed*, yes; but overwhelmed, less so.)

When our initial enthusiasm for nature in theory collides with
the real thing, it is hard not to feel daunted. A metaphorical skip into
the delights of the outdoors becomes a slow crash of realization . . .
'Is there no end to all this random matter?' This is a normal reaction and not an unhealthy one. It does at least mean we have noticed
some of the detail in our surroundings, but it also hints at the challenge ahead.

If we look at one example from the plant kingdom, and then one from the animal, we will see the scale of this challenge.

Orchids are one member of one branch of the flower family. There are 25,000 different species of orchid alone. No typo, *25k*. If, each day, you took it upon yourself to study and understand one orchid, it would take 68.5 years before you had covered this one species. You could then move on to the daisies.

In 1995 a team of scientists travelled to Panama and studied a group of nineteen trees, looking for beetles. They found them. The scientists identified 1,200 species of beetles, and of these, 960 were new to science.

There really is a lot of stuff out there.

How do we begin to convert a sense of being daunted into one of connection? The key is to start at the opposite end of the scale. We must forget individual species to begin with, and focus our interest more broadly. By building a simple collection of general insights, and leaving species out of the mix for now, the outdoors morphs from *stuff* to *shape*, and from seeming randomness to apparent patterns. Think of the progression in this way:

Initial confusion → Recognizing landscapes and habitats → Knowing what to expect in each habitat → Recognizing fine connections and any anomalies

In this chapter we are going to look at a total of fifteen building blocks. If these are new to you, that might seem like a lot. But give them a chance, as they can help explain almost everything you see in nature. Besides, the alternative is to start at page 1 of an orchid book that weighs half a ton.

Let's start with some of the simplest of these building blocks:

1.   All animals, humans included, need water. Water sources increase the local populations of animals, and the presence of animals often indicates the presence of water nearby. London would not exist without the Thames.

2.   Plants can survive on basic chemical nutrients – air, sunlight and minerals – but all animals need to eat other living things. They need food in the form of plants or other animals.

3.   Animals that eat plants tend towards living in groups: there is usually no shortage of plant matter, and they benefit from having more eyes to look out for predators.

4.   Predators tend to work alone if they are going for small prey or in packs if they are going after very large prey.

Now we can deduce that if we see an animal, it follows that there must be some water and a specific food source in the form of a plant or another animal very nearby. If we add some more building blocks the picture starts to get a little more interesting:

5.   In the wild, given enough time, trees will come to dominate all land, outside of extreme regions like the Arctic or high mountains.

6. Most plants, including young trees, cannot survive being bitten down to ground level. Grasses are one of the most significant exceptions: their bud – the part of the plant needed for new growth – is below the surface and survives grazing.

7. Life is tough for all wild plants and animals, and they are very sensitive to their environment. They have each evolved to out-compete other species if environmental conditions – i.e. habitat – are suitable, but struggle if they are not.

The simple concepts above explain the appearance of the landscapes we see.

Exercise 12

In this exercise we are going to see building-block 5 in action.

Look at the photo of a mountain below. Notice the way you can spot different habitats as you look from the bottom to the top. Deciduous trees thrive in the warm sheltered valley, these give way to conifers a little higher up, then a little higher the conditions are too hard and all the trees give up at the 'treeline'. Above this, the hardier shrubs like gorse and heather take over, and going higher still, only the hardiest grasses survive and these will continue up to the snowline, if a mountain is high enough. Each plant has thrived within its own microhabitat, and none of them could survive within each other's for long.

Plant life changes dependably with altitude, giving us nature's altimeter.

The beauty of this simple way of looking at habitats on a mountain is that it will work all over the world, with no knowledge of individual species. It is one of the best ways of forming a small instant connection with a landscape. In natural navigation terms, this is nature's altimeter.

Before agriculture came onto the scene about six thousand years ago, woodland dominated the British Isles. To look after livestock and sow crops, it was necessary to clear the woodland. The result is what we see today, a tussle between humans, woodland, edible crops, grazing animals and grasses.

The next time you pass through a variety of inland rural land-scapes in a car or train, notice how every single one of these landscapes can be explained by the principles above.

Everywhere you look, you will see one or more of four things:

1. Woodland
2. Crops being farmed
3. Animals grazing grasses
4. Built-up areas

This is the first stage in identifying habitats. It sounds obvious, and it is, but there is an important distinction between seeing a sheep and understanding a sheep's place in the scheme of things. The person whose thought process stops with the less-than-dramatic thought, 'There is a sheep and some trees', has clearly not made the same connection with their surroundings as the person who thinks: 'There is a sheep; it is a herbivore and likes to live in a flock; there are likely to be lots more. There they are. I wonder why there is a small copse of young trees in the middle of their grassy field? Oh I see now, there is a fence around it stopping the sheep grazing there and killing the saplings . . . But, I wonder why the farmer fenced this area off in the first place . . .'

Once we are used to seeing the landscape as a series of habitats, we can begin to ask and answer more interesting questions. And we will find a large number of the answers by thinking about water and rocks.

First we need to clear up a big misconception. There is a temptation to think of places as being different because they are in different places. The Lake District is like the Lake District because it is . . . the Lake District. Yosemite National Park is like Yosemite National Park because it is Yosemite National Park. Beneath the ludicrousness of these statements lurks something big and key.

Rocks and water explain a lot about every natural environment, regardless of where they are. Time for our final set of building blocks:

8. All land is based on rocks of some kind.

9. Some rocks, like chalk, are porous and some, like slate, are non-porous. Non-porous rocks hold water above them and lead to wet areas. Porous rocks let the water filter down through them and lead to dry areas.

10. Some plants and animals like wet conditions and some like drier conditions.

11. Some rocks, like granite, lead to soil above them that is acidic and some, like chalk, form soil that is alkaline.

12. Most plants prefer alkaline conditions, so you get more plants and more diverse plants growing in areas with alkaline soils.

13. Rivers carve V-shaped valleys and meander, creating interlocking spurs that result in restricted views. During the last ice age, on the other hand, glaciers carved big, wide U-shaped valleys with great views.

14. Where the sea meets land, the wind creates waves and constant erosion. Depending on the rocks it acts upon, this process gives us beaches, cliffs and many more beguiling landforms.

15. The side of a landmass closest to the sea, in the direction the wind comes from, will get most of the rain. The weather in the UK arrives from the west: Wales is a lot wetter than East Anglia, which is on average 34 per cent drier than the rest of England and Wales.

Granted, that's quite a few building blocks, but by using them you can not only understand habitats, but you can predict the things you will find in them. This is because once you are aware of these very broad characteristics – acid or alkaline, wet or dry, river or glacier country – then suddenly the green chaos starts to organize itself before your eyes.

The habits of some familiar animals and plants are well known to us. For instance, most people know that cows are rarely found in the middle of the woods, but that shade-loving fungi thrive there.

Quite quickly, we can appreciate that every single animal and plant is an 'indicator' of some sort; it is trying to tell us something about the environment. Frogs and dragonflies live in still, freshwater habitats, so you will not find them far from lakes and ponds. Some plants, like heather, love direct sunlight, so you will tend to find them on south-facing slopes. Once we add all these indicators together we form a beautifully intricate picture of the place where we find ourselves. And the reason we find ourselves there is not usually a coincidence; it is connected to the landscape's intricacy.

The Lake District in the UK is a popular destination, and its many visitors go there not because it is conveniently situated, but – indirectly – because it is comprised of a lot of non-porous rocks and has been shaped by glaciers. The glacial ice formed big U-shaped valleys, and the water that collects in these valleys can't get down through the rocks at the bottom and so collects to form picturesque lakes. The poetry of Wordsworth, Coleridge and hundreds of others has been inspired by the Lake District's dramatic views, and these have been sculpted by rocks, ice and water.

Granite creates acidic soils and is non-porous, so we find wet inhospitable conditions above granite. Mosses are one of the few plants that can thrive in such conditions, and over many years the mosses are compressed down to form peat. So, granite creates a boggy, peaty wilderness we have come to call a moor. Dartmoor is the way it is because of the granite below the surface.

The sorts of habitats we are likely to encounter are:

- Grasslands
- Shrublands
- Woodlands
- Wetlands
- Coastal
- Rocky
- Artificial – from farmland to urban

Within each of these, the rock below the surface and the actions of the water on that rock will create more specific types of habitat. Limestone will support deciduous forests, while sandy soils often lie under pine forests.

The reward for recognizing habitats is that this makes the next stage in connecting with nature much more straightforward. Habitats are like large houses with several extended families living in them. We know that when we go to visit Aunt Jane, there is a high probability that we will also see Uncle John. And so it is with wild habitats: if we are on a chalk hill we can expect to see beech trees, which love alkaline conditions and dry soils, but we should not expect to see many alder trees, which hate dry soil and love their roots to be surrounded by water.

Soon the tangled masses we once saw are revealed as part of a simple system. Instead of feeling overwhelmed, we see order; the plants and animals not only sort themselves into easy-to-understand groups, but allow us to have a lot of fun in making predictions and doing detective work.

Exercise 13

Now it is your turn. Think back to the field with the sheep and the fenced-off young trees. After a squint through the train's window you notice that the field is lined with beech trees, but the fenced-off trees in the middle are alders. Use the information in this chapter to predict one flying creature you might encounter, if you walked from the edge to the centre of the field in summer.

Answer: The alders in the centre of the field hint that there is water there. The farmer has probably fenced off a pond to keep livestock safely out of it. This has also kept the grazing sheep away from the vulnerable saplings and allowed the young alders to thrive. You might encounter a number of flying insects in these conditions, but the one hinted at earlier in this chapter was dragonflies.

The sheep explain the landscape. The chalk explains the beech trees, but the alders hint at a different microhabitat, and this in turn suggests the animals we might encounter. The network is slowly building.

4. The Finer Connections

*'It is possible to spend a lifetime in a magellanic voyage
around the trunk of a single tree.'*
(EDWARD O. WILSON)

We tend to become familiar with our home habitats first and the
regulars that will be found there. This familiarity is what makes it
easy to spot change. Think of your favourite song, one you know off
by heart and have listened to a thousand times. If an artist released
a remix of this song, the change would be instantly noticeable to you
– it might even jar. But to someone who was unfamiliar with the
original, the new version would be harder to distinguish. Once we
learn to recognize the background sounds, we start to pick out each
new note instinctively.

I live in the South Downs; it is chalk country and beech forests
abound. Inevitably, I have become familiar with the dependable
cohorts of these shady woodlands: grey squirrels, deer, pheasants,
orchids and the beech-loving fungi, like the saffrondrop bonnet,
Mycena crocata. These organisms form the expected canvas, but
I will be quickly intrigued by anything that stands out as less than
common. A pheasant will not drag my eyes upwards for long, but a
white-tailed eagle would.

Nature is a series of specialists and their partners. Fungi and
forests work in tandem; vast subterranean networks of fungi fix

nitrogen for the trees that offer the perfect habitat for them. If we spot the specialist, we will likely find the partner. For example, the cinnabar moth caterpillar can only feed on ragwort, so if we spot one, we can be confident of finding the other.

From the rodents that colonize the London Underground, through the 'railway poplars' that screen many urban railway lines, to the bright green lichens that cling to the wind-scoured rocks of the mountains of north Wales – no habitat is off-limits to the inquisitive mind looking for specialist species. Studies have been done into the microhabitats that are cemeteries and, rather wonderfully for lovers of all things vampire, these areas have been found to offer important insect-rich feeding areas for bats.

If you spend enough time in a place, the regulars introduce themselves, and their reason for choosing that place is usually easy to work out. Sometimes it is a little trickier, but then the sport of puzzle-solving commences. There is a peculiar satisfaction in cracking nature's riddles: why do these pigeons always use exactly the same flightpath? Aha! They are following the road below. Pigeons, like many other birds, follow lines in the ground like motorways and rivers.

When the shapes and colours of a habitat become familiar to us and the individual species attract our curiosity, we will be confronted with an important and much-dreaded hurdle: species identification and names. More people have felt an early interest in nature snuffed out by the tyranny of species names than probably any other single factor.

Depending on your experience, you may have sensed a mild dismay on encountering the Latin name of the fungus, *Mycena crocata*, at the start of this chapter. I deliberately squeezed it in there to help make this point. I don't know whether it is the way many subjects are taught at school that sows a long-term loathing of such things, but most people find subjects with a lot of new names forbidding. The study of the natural world is absolutely stuffed with them: common names, Latin names, nicknames and names that are impossible to pronounce. But however unpalatable the words *Mycena crocata* may be at first, we do need some way of differentiating between species.

If names feel like a stumbling block, then there are a couple of fun ways around this problem. Firstly, banish fear of getting something wrong, because it is impossible. There are no rights or wrongs, just invented words. Names are a convention, a very useful one for many of us at times, but if they are not proving useful for you at any one time, then they serve no purpose at that moment. The only time you are likely to fear getting a name wrong is when you are trying to convey the identity of something to another person, and there are many other ways of doing this. If you want to call something 'that stringy green thingy with a white flower that looks like a gramophone', then that is as correct as calling it hedge bindweed or *Convolvulus sepium*, for that matter. After a few times using that long expression, you may start to see a little beauty in the shorter names, but if not, so be it!

Sadly, the natural world is not short of people who believe that rattling off Latin names incessantly makes them appear clever, whereas most of us know instinctively that this suggests insecurity at best, but possibly social and sexual dysfunction as well. If somebody corrects you sternly by using an obtuse name for something, they probably know neither human nature nor any other kind very profoundly.

When I teach people how to use the stars to find their way, one of the first things I say is, 'Shapes and the way these shapes move in the sky are very important for natural navigators. Names never have been and never will be. Call it the Plough, the Big Dipper, the Saucepan or part of Ursa Major – you will not change the way it looks or the way it can be used to find the North Star.'

The second fun way to beat names at their own game is to don a deerstalker hat, light a pipe and enjoy the clues within. The common names of most plants and animals will contain interesting indicators as to the characteristics of their owners, and these can offer rewarding insight. Instead of viewing names as an obstacle to experience, with practice they come to be seen as a gateway. The saffrondrop bonnet fungus mentioned earlier bleeds a rich orange when bruised, and once you have seen the gore of this orange blood you are unlikely to forget this fungus or its name quickly.

Names are dead words until we find meaning in them, but as soon as we do, the species behind them can find new life in our imagination. Take the words 'ghost orchid'. We may know what an orchid is and we may be familiar, from *Scooby Doo* if nowhere else, with what a ghost is. However, 'ghost orchid' isn't likely to stick in our minds for long unless we find some meaning to that pairing. If a friend returns from a walk in the woods and announces that they saw a roe deer, a brown owl and a ghost orchid, then they may possibly be a little underwhelmed by our response of, 'That's nice.'

Once we learn that ghost orchids earned their name because they are one of the rarest plants in Britain and can disappear from a site for whole decades at a time, before reappearing briefly, the name comes to life a bit. The next time someone announces they have seen

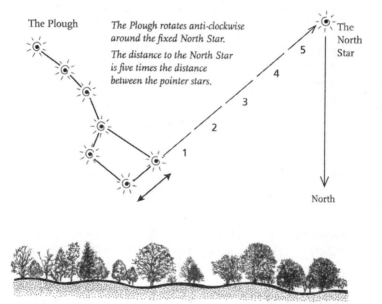

The Plough

The Plough rotates anti-clockwise around the fixed North Star.

The distance to the North Star is five times the distance between the pointer stars.

The North Star

North

Finding the North Star.

a ghost orchid, we can oblige them by falling off our chair in the expected manner.

It is a privilege to see a very rare plant or animal, but that does not on its own give us a connection. It might be a good idea for us to draw a couple of the strands together at this point. Imagine you are walking down a country lane in May and someone next to you points to a yellow flower and says, 'Look, St John's wort is out already,' you should not feel ashamed to find yourself unmoved. Nor is there any need to offer a gruff retort in the form of, 'Do I look bothered?' Instead, take a moment to look at the flower, enjoy peering at its little yellow spikes and then, at your leisure, investigate the name. The next time you walk down that same country lane you will be able to turn to a new walking companion and explain that St John's wort earned its name because it was traditionally known to flower on St John's day, 24 June. The flower's Latin name, *Hypericum perforatum*, makes more sense once you have held one of its leaves up to the light. They have small oil glands in them, which do give them a perforated appearance. The word *Hypericum* comes from the Greek words *hyper* and *eikon*, 'above' and 'picture', from the tradition of hanging a plant over a picture to ward off evil on St John's Day, this being a plant that has a reputation for doing just that. St John's wort is widely used to treat depression, and there is scientific evidence backing its use for certain cases.

If your friend finds this interesting, you might choose to reveal the fruits of your further research. It was once believed that a child-less woman could walk out naked to pick the St John's wort flower, and this would lead to her conceiving within a year. And if your friend raises an eyebrow, you might add, 'However, it is possible that

The elusive ghost orchid.

the flower played only a small part in these fertility trials: walking about naked in midsummer might have been a good way of introducing new mates into the equation. Varieties like winter heliotrope are unlikely to have earned such a reputation, as naked rambling in December might be considered mad, not licentious.'

By this point there is a danger that your companion will be making judgments about your own social skills, so it will be time to move on to the next exhibit.

You will, however, have demonstrated to your own satisfaction that, with a little curiosity, dead words spring to life and the name of this one plant allows us to feel a connection with history, medicine and sex. The name has allowed it to metamorphose in our minds from a yellow flower into a calendar and then a pharmacy.

Nature is often like a painting that seems dull until you start to learn more about it. Van Gogh added yet more piquancy to the vibrancy of his art by cutting off part of his ear. His paintings change in our minds, without changing physically, when we learn more about the story that surrounds them.

Take a look at the two flightless birds on the opposite page and assess how you feel looking at these two creatures. Granted these are motionless black-and-white photographs, but it is hard to feel for either subject in each case.

Let me give you a little backstory on these two birds. The first, the male emperor penguin, will allow his hungry partner to go off and feed after she has laid the egg, while he fasts so that he can protect their egg for four months. He will endure winds of 120 mph and temperatures that fall to lower than −40°c. He is the only male penguin to do this without help from the female.

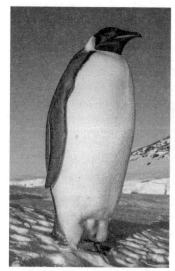

A penguin and a cassowary. Do you feel anything?

The second, the cassowary, is another large flightless bird. Its second 'toe' is a lethal nail-like spike that can tear flesh – a cassowary once killed a 16-year-old boy by piercing his neck. Look back at the photographs. It is a little easier to feel something with some background. You can see it in their eyes now, can't you?

No longer intimidated by apparent disorder, it is time to heighten the senses, to detect the anomalous: peer deeper, listen more hungrily and sniff for change. We are at the stage where we can look forward to fresh discoveries, to finding new keys to unlock our surroundings.

The competitive pressure of survival is tough on new life, but kind to the naturalist, because it means that each species we find has a story to reveal about the place where we stand and the time we spend there. If we walk through a dense woodland we will not be surprised to find plants that can thrive in the shade. In spring we might be treated to a carpet of bluebells, but alert senses may help us to spot stronger clues to time and place.

The winter aconite flower is an early bloomer, as its name suggests, but getting to know this flower reveals more than a clue to the time of year. If, peering closely, we notice its petals furled in the early morning and unfurled in the afternoon, we can take some satisfaction in having observed one of nature's many thermometers: the winter aconite's petals only open when the air temperature rises above 10°c.

In another patch we may find wood anemone, wood sorrel and woodruff. Each of these plants is a poor colonizer and together they indicate that a woodland habitat is ancient. A picture begins to build of place and time, one that has always been there, but which is seen by few, or, as the French philosopher Henri Bergson put it, 'Disorder is simply the order we are not looking for.'

Our senses can also reveal which animals have come to share each moment with us. There is a strong tradition of 'birding by ear', that is, identifying birds by their calls and then building a picture of a territory by the sounds of the birds. This may sound steeply technical at first, but it is accessible and fun to try. The full art takes years to hone, but the general approach can be understood with the help of a few words. The yellowhammer calls with a rhythm that can be evoked with the sentence, 'a little bit of bread and no cheese'.

Strange, but you get the sound-picture. And the name-detective in you may already have deduced that this is indeed a bird with yellow feathers: *hama* is an Old English word for skin, covering or feathers.

There are other word games that can help us build a different picture. 'Richard of York Gave Battle in Vain' will win few prizes as a history lesson, but it works better as a neat way of remembering the red, orange, yellow, green, blue, indigo and violet sequence in a rainbow. No matter how many times I see a rainbow, I still love checking the outcome of that particular conflict. History does indeed repeat itself.

Ears and eyes cocked to the skies for birdsong and rainbows, we may find our feet trying to tell us about a much smaller creature. It is common in summer to find a stickiness on the ground under Lime trees. This is the work of the aphids that gorge on the tree's sap and then drop the excess sugars below them as a honeydew. There are moulds that thrive on these sugars and form dark patches on cars that park regularly under lime trees. Note to selves: do not park under trees with leaves that are heart-shaped with toothed edges.

Almost everything that our senses pick out is eager to tell us a story that will help us make a connection. The constellation Hercules is itching to boast all about the times he slayed a lion, an eagle and a swan. These victims will be found in the nearby constellations of Leo, Aquila and Cygnus. The plant Danish scurvy-grass, which tolerates salt, earned its name after it was eaten by sailors returning from long periods at sea to satisfy their mortal craving for vitamin C. It has more recently come to colonize the verges of major roads, where we have accidentally created coastal conditions by spreading salt in winter.

It does not take an encyclopaedic list to demonstrate that these finer connections are out there, everywhere, waiting for us to find them. The important thing for us to remember is that nature is a set of keys and interlocking connections. It sometimes takes a little patience to work out how to open a new lock, but the keys are there and the reward on the other side is a recipe for a form of alchemy. Once we see the way all of nature is interconnected we have a way of turning time in the fresh air into a richness of experience. And, unlike the alchemy of old, it works.

5. The Beauty of Conflict

Sweet are the uses of adversity,
Which, like the toad, ugly and venomous,
Wears yet a precious jewel in his head.
(*As You Like It*, ACT II, SCENE I, WILLIAM SHAKESPEARE)

Each species that thrives is well suited to its environment, but this is not a situation that has been arrived at by benign committee. It is the result of violent, unceasing conflict.

Parasitoid wasps lay eggs in caterpillars and then paralyse their host with a poison. The wasp eggs hatch within the caterpillar, then slowly begin to eat it, but they like to keep their victim alive for as long as possible. They start eating the fatty parts of the caterpillar first, then move on to some of the organs, leaving the central nervous system and heart until last.

Sparrowhawks spear pretty tits, and even those models of outdoors citizenry, trees, devise ingenious manoeuvres to outwit each other, each one responding to the shade of their neighbours as they grow. This is not a game.

In 1685 a clan chief from the island of North Rona in the Hebrides returned from time at sea to find that his once-busy home island was desolate. A single lonely and skeletal woman greeted him on the beach, and he soon learned that the rest of his people had starved to death. Somehow, black rats had found their way onto the island and into the islanders' vital food stores. In the battle for resources we call winter, the rats had won.

For tens of thousands of years human beings woke in the morning with a simple game plan: win today's wrestle with nature and tomorrow can take care of itself. Now that we have proved to ourselves that we can temporarily beat nature in almost any game, we have been left with strange new challenges and quandaries. Or perhaps this environmental anxiety is nature's most recent cunning ploy: to wrack humans with existential angst so severe that we are eventually pinned down by vines and creepers and then devoured by crows and worse. Time will tell.

We may find conflict unattractive as a concept, repellent even, but as a mechanism for helping us to connect with nature it is so powerful that it holds a beauty. It is not the conflict itself that will draw us in, but the inevitability that we will find ourselves rooting for one side. Watching my dog walk around our back garden could get boring. Watching one of our chickens potter in one corner of the garden is no more exciting. But running like a maniac to stop my dog from attacking a chicken that has escaped is far from boring.

News of a knife fight in a distant town is less interesting to the average person than hearing that there has been a squabble between two close relatives. It is likely that a ripple in our own pond will be more significant to us than a great wave in the wider ocean. The knife fight makes the news, because the news is a collection of intense conflict stories. Even the good news tends to be moderated conflict, for instance someone triumphing in a sporting event by thrashing everyone else.

The variable element that will decide whether a tussle draws us in and encourages us to form a connection will be our level of interest in the individuals or teams concerned. The great naturalist Aldo Leopold summed this concept up concisely and with a breathtaking political incorrectness, even for 1949: 'A dead Chinaman is of little import to us whose awareness of things Chinese is bounded by an occasional dish of chow mein.'

The nature stories that become best known are the conflicts that resonate most strongly and widely.

Imagine standing at a window in a town and seeing a squirrel climbing a tree. No connection so far. But then you notice that it is unusually red, and this reminds you of one of the best-known nature conflicts of our islands.

The grey squirrel was introduced to Britain in 1876. In the early days, they were a rare and welcome sight and they earned lots of fans. Signs appeared in parks with the words, 'The public are earnestly requested not to molest the grey squirrels.'

Leaving to one side for a moment the arresting image of what a squirrel-molester might look like, we move on only forty years to find a very different official stance. Grey squirrels had rapidly out-competed the home side of red squirrels and bred with such vigour that 4,000 were killed in Kew Gardens and the species was deterred from Royal Parks.

The battle for resources continued through the twentieth century. In 1955, reds were spotted in thirty-three parks in Sheffield. By 1965 they were counted in only four, and 1970 was the last recorded instance of an urban red-squirrel sighting.

So now . . . imagine you see a red-coloured squirrel climbing a tree from your town window.

There are other recent big nature stories that are also steeped in conflict. Think of the elms that have been whittled away by Dutch elm disease in recent decades and, at the time of writing, the fear that the ash trees may be about to go the same way at the hands of the fungal disease that is believed to have come from the continent. We live in interesting times if you are a Europhobic arborphile.

The red squirrels and elms have suffered a drastic decline, because they have been confronted with survival challenges and they are yet to arrive at a solution. Evolution is the sadistic headmaster of the Succeed-or-Die School of Invention, motto: *Disce aut consumere!* – 'learn or get eaten!'.

It is sad and sometimes ugly when a species fails in this school, especially ugly if the change they are confronted with is caused by human thoughtlessness. Sometimes the two happen in tandem and ugliness can create unexpected beauty.

New railway lines are notorious for the havoc and destruction they can bring to a landscape, impacting both natural and artificial environments. However, the need to keep general human traffic away from the iron dragons that pass along these new lines has created a new habitat and led to a renaissance in rare wildflowers in some areas. But perhaps the most surreal and ironic example of this is the fact that many naturalists now support the military's habit of firing big explosive shells at landscapes. Exploding ordnance falling from the sky has the dependable effect of keeping humans away and, consequently, firing ranges from Devon to Scotland have accidentally created some of the most healthy ecosystems in Britain. Naturalists and the military are now working more closely, and this unlikely partnership is becoming less accidental and more deliberate.

Danger for humans can spell good news for the rest of nature.

Nothing intensifies our interest in nature like the subject of human influence: for example, economic growth and planning permission versus ancient woodlands and protected birds. Roll up, roll up, ringside seats available . . . Be warned, by the second round you will probably want to climb between the ropes and give one side a broken nose. Try thinking of your favourite open space and saying the following words dispassionately: 'My favourite place to go for a walk may not be ideally suited to a new supermarket.'

Some of nature's most intriguing displays come when a species prevails in the face of an evolutionary challenge. The carnivorous pitcher plant, *Nepenthes pervillei*, lures insects into a fluid-filled cup. There they die in an acid bath. Grotesque, effective and simple, so far, but evolution never stands still. Large insects cause the plant problems and foul up its digestive system. There is only one ant that can survive this heinous environment, and it is also the only ant that can swim, the *Colobopsis* ant. This ant feeds on those larger insects that would otherwise cause problems for the plant. Evolution is exquisite: it creates one ant that can not only swim, but chooses to do its lengths in an acid bath that kills pretty much everything else its size. Here, the ant serenely eats lunch in the shade provided by its gruesome, murderous host.

Lettuces form a good lunch for many aphids, but once the lettuces realize they are being attacked by the bingeing aphids, they begin to manufacture a poison to deter them. Thus evolution has devised a cunning counterattack method for the lettuce. This is great, but wouldn't it be so much better if the plants could detect an attack by an animal *before* it was launched? Yes, of course, but how could that be possible? The genius of evolution is best seen when it solves problems that humans might struggle with. Think for a moment how you would give a plant a system that allowed it to predict that an animal attack was imminent. Bear in mind that plants have no brain.

Scientists have worked out that many plants are able to protect themselves from animal attack by staying finely tuned to the chemicals being produced by other plants. Incredibly, we now know that a plant can pre-empt an attack by an animal, long before it has been attacked itself, by *'chemical eavesdropping'*. If a poplar tree picks up the scent of other trees being attacked by insects, it produces more of the toxic compounds that inhibit the growth of its enemy, the caterpillar, long before the creatures launch their offensive on that particular tree.

In any closely matched battle, an arms race of ingenuity is likely. One of the most fun examples of this can be found in the tussle between a giant mammal and a tree. Giraffes in Botswana eat the leaves of acacia trees. The acacia tree is not keen on being completely devoured, and so releases tannins to deter the giraffes. This chemical messenger is picked up by other trees, which pre-empt attack and produce the chemical in anticipation. How do you think the giraffes beat this system?

The giraffes have learned to eat the acacias starting at the downwind end of a group of acacias. What will the acacias 'think' of next?

Conflict in the natural world is not limited to organism versus organism. Life for many creatures and plants is a regular battle against the elements, and many animals find particular seasons precarious. If, during the lean months, the smallest birds encounter

What will the acacias 'think' of next?

a source of food, they must regulate their intake: too little and they will starve, too much and they lose agility and are likely to fall prey.

The changing seasons mark a constant shift in opportunities and challenges for most species. It is not as simple as 'summer good, winter bad'. While winter means depleted food and harsher weather, many parasites and diseases flourish in the warmth and humidity of summer. Predators and prey find their odds alter with changes in temperature, foliage, food-scarcity, water levels, light levels and their own populations. There is a tendency for us to back the underdog when the going is tough, which is probably why it is so exciting to watch prey escaping during such times. A fall of snow will make it harder for prey like rabbits to hide; who wouldn't cheer for a rabbit running over snow ahead of a dog? Not everyone would; that's what makes it interesting.

Animals have numerous systems for warning them of attack by other animals – from the neighbourhood-watch system of birds, who make others of their kind aware of danger with their alarm calls, to the small mammals that beat the ground as a warning drum. Nor should we be surprised to find animals and plants communicating with each other about impending battles with the weather. Scientists have noted that pine and oak trees emit ultrasonic vibrations during a drought, as their water-bearing vessels respond to the decrease in available water, and it has even been suggested that other trees are picking up on these signals somehow.

An appreciation that conflict is an inevitable part of nature can help us to notice and then connect with the supersensitive balance in an area. Any tweak to any variable will tip some species into the ascendant and others into trouble.

The constant challenge of survival, the same one our not-so-distant ancestors struggled with, might also be the reason why we abhor excessive violence. There is a difference between the demands of survival and gratuitous killing. The fox that systematically slaughters all the chickens and leaves most of them dead, instead of killing and taking just one, makes few friends. The writer Roger Deakin was incensed by the squirrels that laid waste to an excessive number of his walnuts, likening them to the thieves that vandalize a home after burgling it: 'Grow up, act your age. Just take what you need and bugger off.'

Noticing the mass conflict around us and finding ourselves taking sides in small battles is an integral part of forming a connection with nature. Anyone who denies this is still waiting to form a connection. We can remain impartial from a distance, but the sight of abundant death has a way of triggering a measure of empathy which grows into a connection, and with this comes a strong interest in the wellbeing of certain animals or plants. The further away the battles take place, the bigger they need to be for most people to become connected. This is why we hear stories about local species, but distant ecosystems.

We may feel moved by the plight of the whole Amazon rainforest or the single rare bird that visited our back yard once. Scale and proximity will have a bearing on which conflicts trigger our emotions, but once we take sides it is inevitable that we will feel a connection.

IV. Getting Closer

1. Hidden Calendars

'The Sun, with all those planets revolving around it and dependent on it, can still ripen a bunch of grapes as if it had nothing else to do.'

(GALILEO GALILEI)

Five hundred years ago, a young girl called Pepita lived in a small village in Mexico. On Christmas Eve, Pepita made her way to church with the other children from the village. She could see that all the others were carrying beautiful gifts for the baby Jesus. Pepita was sad as she did not have enough money to buy even the smallest of gifts for Jesus. Pepita's cousin, Pedro, put his arm around her shoulders as they walked together,

'Don't worry, Pepita, even the most humble gift, if given in love, will be acceptable in the Lord's eyes.'

Pepita bent down and gathered a small bunch of the green weeds that lined the lane. At the church she placed the green plants at the altar and said her prayers. The other children laughed at her.

'Do you think Jesus wants your weeds, Pepita?'

Pepita cried and ran out of the church. She sat on her own and wept, listening to her friends singing inside. Then she walked home all alone.

On Christmas Day, Pepita and Pedro walked to the church together again, but Pepita refused to go in.

'You go, Pedro, the others will just laugh at me because I am so poor.'

Pedro could not persuade his cousin to join him in the church and he went inside, leaving Pepita sitting all alone outside once more.

Then Pedro rushed out.

'Come, Pepita, come! Quick!'

Pedro led his cousin back inside the church and pointed towards the altar. The green plants had turned a vibrant red and the whole congregation stood in silence. They were staring in amazement.

The legend of the poinsettia miracle, like all good legends, contains kernels of truth and insight. Poinsettias are 'short-day' plants, which means they are very sensitive to the number of hours of consecutive darkness they are exposed to.

As the nights lengthen towards the end of the year, poinsettias turn red. It is actually the leaves of the plant that change colour, although the effect is so vivid that they are regularly confused with flowers.

The poinsettia has become a plant that is symbolic of Christmas in many parts of the world, and in their native Mexico poinsettias are known as 'Flores de Noche Buena', 'Flowers of Christmas Eve'. Commercial growers will manipulate the time at which the plants turn red by controlling the length of night artificially. Home growers can accelerate the change in a similar way, by placing the plants in a dark place – a church, in Pepita's case.

Contained within this legend are the keys that help make some sense of time. What is time? What is a year? Is it 365 days, or twelve months or a financial-accounting period? Or is it a succession of changes that surround us: frosts followed by snowdrops, primroses, bluebells, leaves on the trees, cuckoos, swallows, wildflowers, berries, fungi, turning leaves, gales and another frost?

Or is a year closer to this: central heating, flood warnings, flu, treacherous roads, clocks going forward, Easter eggs, the football season ending, a beach holiday, the football season starting again, clocks going back, kids playing conkers (in magazines but nowhere else), time to buy a new coat, Christmas?

The way we view a year is a good measure of our connection with nature, because a failure to notice dramatic change is symptomatic of a relationship that is on weak ground. Think of the person who goes on a health drive, loses a stone, changes their hairstyle, gets a spray-on tan one morning and buys a whole new wardrobe that afternoon. If this scale of change goes unnoticed by their other half, this is a relationship that may be in some peril.

One annoying mistake that a lot of nature enthusiasts make is to cajole people to appreciate the changing seasons. What a waste of everybody's time that sort of sentiment is. Yes, nature's seasonal displays are the greatest shows on earth, but we can only come to love and understand them by getting to know the minor characters. Trying to take in the whole show in one go is the sort of challenge that God might find entertaining, but even He would probably feel the need for a sit down with a cup of tea and a biscuit afterwards.

As we saw in the previous chapters, we can start to make sense of the vast canvas around us by moving from the big relationships, the broad brushstrokes of habitat-knowledge, to the finer connections, the species within those habitats. This narrowing from broad to fine focus is what allows us to make sense of our natural surroundings in the moment. This approach helps us to make decisions about the aspects of the nature matrix that we find most intriguing. The area we end up taking most interest in comes down to a personal decision – birds are no better than bees, bass or buddleias – but once made, it is this interest in a particular area that allows us to begin to unravel the melees of change that are the seasons.

Every meaningful gauge of time will find its roots in the daily revolution of the earth, the annual orbit of the earth around the sun and the regular changes in weather, plant and animal life patterns that follow as a consequence. While nobody is oblivious to the broadest changes in their environment – those that occur between summer and winter – almost everybody has lost contact with the subtler patterns of change that surround us. It does not matter whether we look at the habits of the sun, the night sky or the smallest of plants, we can rediscover lost calendars.

Sky Calendars

Necessity led our ancestors to a very practical relationship with the stars. Sirius is the brightest star in the night sky and the ancient Egyptians used its appearance to predict the annual flood of the Nile. Early cultures across the world found their patterns of life tied to what they saw above them: aboriginal Australians traditionally began cultivation when the Pleiades, or the 'Seven Sisters', appeared.

If we are keen to regain this lost connection with time in the night sky, then language can help. Sometimes the clues in the names of shapes in the sky are obvious, like the Summer and Winter Triangles; sometimes they require a little more thought and cultural immersion. Virgo is usually depicted holding an ear of corn, symbolizing summer. Aries is the ram, ancient symbol of fertility and hence a spring constellation.

Natural navigators have to learn quickly that the sun rises and sets in a slightly different place each day and this direction varies massively over the course of a year. In midwinter in the UK, the sun rises in the southeast and sets in the southwest, but in midsummer the sun rises in the northeast and sets in the northwest. When it comes to sunrise and sunset, time and direction are two sides of the same coin; if you know one then you can deduce the other. The ancients approached this relationship from the opposite side to the navigator. If you wish to learn how to use the sun as a calendar, then it is a good idea to emulate the ancients in their approach.

If you mark the point where the sun rises over the course of a year using stones viewed from a fixed point, then you have a calendar. We can find these calendars still standing, both in places with names that are familiar, like Stonehenge, and in less familiar locations spread across the Bronze Age landscape. If you can see either sunrise or sunset from the same place over the course of half a year or more, then this is something it is well worth trying yourself. There is no need to haul giant stones to the summit of a hill; marks on a windowsill can create the same effect, and an equally accurate calendar.

The Ring of Brodgar at sunset, Orkney, Scotland. Any structures that line up with the sunrise or sunset like this, however modest, create a calendar.

Ground Time

Even the shortest walk can be a tour of wondrous natural calendars, clocks and thermometers. Most plants stop growing below about 6°c, but each plant and animal will respond to light and temperature in a unique way, which can be read with practice.

At its simplest level this process begins with the realization that there are windows of opportunity whatever our interests are. Flowers, fish, fungi and fowl will make it quite clear to us early on that they have a calendar and a schedule. Part of becoming a nature-lover is a reconciling of diaries. Sometimes this can be done casually – we look out for the first swallows each year in a laid-back way – but occasionally, a more formal arrangement is needed. The reindeer in Lapland begin their summer migration with an eerie punctiliousness: they set off on 29 July each year.

There isn't a scientist on earth who could possibly offer insight into even 10 per cent of the natural global change that takes place during the course of one year, and yet every single person who develops a connection with nature will be able to relate some of the annual narrative within their area of interest. And these stories will get more detailed with each passing year.

If, for example, we develop an interest in trees, this will inevitably start with an awareness of the most dramatic patterns: spring leaf growth and autumnal shedding. Before long, curiosity will have revealed that plants are sensitive to the length of night, and that it is this that gives them an 'awareness' of season. (Commercial strawberry growers like to put the light on in the middle of the night; five minutes is all it takes to turn one long night into two short ones for the plants. Winter becomes summer at the flick of a switch.)

During the following year of tree-watching, the golds and reds of falling leaves may reveal yet more interest behind the beauty, because we have learned that the trees use this time to filter out toxins, and that any poisonous metals that they have drawn up from the soil during the course of the previous year will be urgently ushered into these falling leaves and sent on their way. The golden leaves take on a fresh metallic sheen in our minds.

My passion for natural navigation means that I have become well versed in the dark and light arts that are phototropism, gravitropism and thigmomorphogenesis (the way plants grow in response to light, gravity and touch respectively). I love using trees as a compass, and this practical curiosity led quickly to a more academic curiosity, because the only way I could answer the questions I had was to learn about the way trees respond to sunlight, gravity, wind and time. (You know you've got the nature bug pretty bad when you're spending evenings reading academic research papers about the weight of tree roots in another country . . . for fun.) This has in turn led me to understand many annual changes in trees, allowing me to connect with time in a deeper and more intriguing way each time I take a walk. At its simplest level, I notice things like the way you can estimate the age of a young conifer tree by counting the number of lateral branch whorls. At a deeper level, I recognize late autumn as the time when I can first read direction from the shape of tree branches at a distance. (Tree branches on the southern side are more horizontal than the northern side, because of phototropism.)

Similarly, an interest in birds will lead to an awareness of the way sensors in a bird's brain respond to varying light levels and times. The migratory habits of birds stimulate our interest in seasonal change

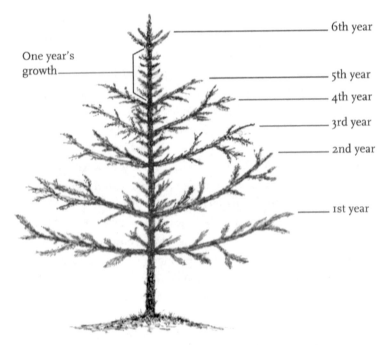

6th year

One year's growth

5th year

4th year

3rd year

2nd year

1st year

How old is this conifer? The levels of branch whorls reveal all.

like nothing else. They come and they go. And in that sentence lie joys and mysteries that have filled a thousand books or more.

Anglers will take great pleasure in knowing the seasonal habits of trout or salmon in a way that might surprise the fish themselves, should a frank discussion between the two camps ever take place.

Each autumn, red admiral butterflies depart our shores for the second-home, sherry-steeped brochure-land of Andalucia in Spain. Here they lay their eggs and die. No species is immune to the rhythms beat out by the sun. We certainly aren't: have you ever tried driving to Cornwall at the start of the summer holidays?

The Rebels

Species that rebel against seasonal norms are loved for their courage. The mistle thrush that can be heard to sing when all other birds have turned shy, even during winter gales, earns our respect, and his nickname, 'stormcock', comes alive on the wind. The red berries and dark-green leaves of holly have found their way onto Christmas cards and earned a little fondness, despite their prickles, because they refuse to let their colours be bowed by a decrease in daylight or a blanket of snow. Gorse will flower at any time of year, and our love of this resilience can be found in the old saying, 'Gorse is out of bloom when kissing's out of fashion'.

If we love the natural rebels, then there are some very mixed feelings about species that have been made to rebel artificially. People might feel differently about the availability of tomatoes in winter if they knew that their ripeness has been achieved by the introduction of cold-resistant genes taken from fish.

It is not only the plants and animals that can rebel. We can, too, by doing things that gently shock the senses. A cold winter night walk can reset the senses and introduce new joys to a landscape that we thought we knew too well.

The things that mark time for us can reveal our interests and, since our interests go some way to defining us, we can learn a lot about a person by asking the question, 'What does spring mean to you?'

Try it on someone if you don't believe me. When they ask what you mean by your question, do not be deterred. Lean forward and repeat your question, speaking clearly and slowly. Now smile and whisper in their ear, 'Spring has come when you can cover seven daisies with one foot.'

And then do a traditional spring fertility dance. This is all essential.

Spring has come when your foot can cover seven daisies.

2. Fast Change

'How can that nasty little machine possibly know what the great golden Sun is up to?'
(OSCAR WILDE)

The writer Jay Griffiths spent six months living with the Karen tribe in Northern Thailand. She was the only one wearing a watch, but bizarrely, she felt she was the only one who could never really tell what the time was. The Karen were sensitive to the shifts in light, temperature and sound, and this gave them a more fundamental understanding of time than a watch could: 'the forest over the course of a day supplied a symphony of time, provided you knew the score.'

This is a beautiful idea, but knowing the score is a bigger challenge than those three words might suggest. I would guess that the Karen themselves don't *know* the 'score'. They have most likely amassed enough experience for their understanding of time to lie deeper in their minds than 'knowledge', which sits closer to the surface. This is a concept that I encounter regularly in navigation: if, from memory, you try to make a list of all the twists and turns you take on a regular long journey, you will almost certainly miss one or two. And yet if you undertake the journey, you do not get lost. Our experience and understanding of many aspects of our surroundings is *contextual*. This book has the words 'How to' at the start of the title, so it is my job to try to shortcut this process of long-term accumulation of experience. Advice like 'go native for five years' would be a lazy and unhelpful solution to this problem. How can we learn to appreciate time like the Karen without turning our lives upside down? Fortunately some practical techniques are available.

In my natural navigation courses I try to make sure that everyone leaves with one question added to their daily routine: 'Which way am I looking?' Answering this question using nature alone will take you on a mental adventure. Time and navigation are very closely related, and my other favourite question is: 'What time is it?' If you attempt to answer these two questions as accurately as possible without using any man-made devices, you will find yourself on a journey, one that takes you from the plants by your feet out into the solar system and beyond. The key is to ask *yourself* those questions. The value lies not in the accuracy of your answers, but in the attempt you make to reach them.

We are all familiar with loose natural time concepts like the well-worn 'dawn chorus' of the birds, but birders develop a way of tuning into this clock more finely. They note the skylark that stops at dusk and starts at dawn, and the progression of early risers that pre-empt even the more famous alarm call of the cockerel.

Today we may develop natural time-telling skills out of desire, but the roots of it lie in practical necessity. The dairy farmers that get up at five every morning do not do it out of a masochistic love of the Shipping Forecast. Their wellingtons tread in the footsteps of ancient, universal traditions. From Rajasthan to Central Africa, pastoral people see time through the rhythms of their animals: the

Konso of Central Africa describe the period we know as 5–6 p.m. as *kakalseema* – 'when the cattle return home'. But what are the cattle tuned into? It is not the atomic clock in Teddington, which counts 9,192,631,770 oscillations of a caesium atom before declaring a second to have passed. The Konso and the cattle's clock is the sun.

Every clock, watch, calendar and diary ever invented by humans does a simple job imperfectly. They each track the earth's daily revolution and its orbit around the sun. They are all wrong most of the time. Midday on a watch is rarely midday. Midday is the middle of the day, the moment that the sun is highest in the sky, not twelve o'clock on a watch. Timepieces can track time and some do a better job than others, but they don't create, define or discover it. Dava Sobel put it well: 'A clock or watch may keep time, but only a sundial can *find* time.'

A watch that disagrees strongly with the sun becomes worthless. The most powerful people on earth will look like fools if they declare it morning before the sun has given permission. For time to have any objective meaning, we must look to the sky. Time is measured by our relationship with the sky, but the word 'our' is important. It is not just how we relate to the sky as individuals or even as a species: in this instance, 'our' refers to all living things. Animals each follow their own daily rhythm, and plants such as Arctic poppies, snow buttercups and many others turn to face towards the sun over the course of each day.

The stars, animals, flowers and sun beat out time with varying degrees of meticulousness. There are also many time clues that are less exact. In many mountainous tropical parts of the world, moist maritime air reaches the hills at midday every day, obscuring the summits in cloud. Or is it ten to twelve? Domestic flights in Sarawak,

Borneo are scheduled in the mornings to beat the dependable afternoon fogs. Fog-, flower- and star-clocks tick around the world.

Even a nature neophyte will be able to tell summer from winter, by assessing the temperature and looking at tree leaves. A nature enthusiast will be able to tell which month it is by observing the birds or the flowers. And a nature zealot may be able to tell the time of day from the opening and closing of a daisy (so named because its petals open and close at dawn and dusk, forming a 'day's eye'). But the most important thing, however deep your commitment, is to try to make a true connection with nature. A sensitivity to the way we can read time in nature leads to an understanding that no two moments are ever repeated. We never see, smell, hear, feel or taste the same thing in exactly the same way twice. This is true in any context, but the importance of it is overlooked by most people outdoors.

Most of us would appreciate that a journey on the Indian Pacific Railway or to see Persepolis would represent a once-in-a-lifetime opportunity. Far fewer recognize that the sight of, for example, a crow flying over a field will never be repeated exactly. There are too many variables. Even if the same crow flew in exactly the same way, the sky, light, colours, plants, scents, temperature and sounds we experienced would all be different. Each time we notice anything outdoors it is a once-in-a-lifetime experience. We have truly learned to read time when we have discovered that nature itself allows us to distinguish each moment from those that come before and after it.

Before Charles I was executed in 1649, his parting gift to his son was the silver sundial he carried with him. For the king, a lump of silver this size was not a significant part of his estate, but the message he meant to pass with it might have been.

V. Real Connection

1. The Clocks Within

'I was out early before breakfast this morning bathing from the sands. There was a delicious feeling of freedom in stripping in the open air and running down naked to the sea, where the waves were curling white with foam and the red morning sunshine glowed upon the naked limbs of the bathers.'

(FRANCIS KILVERT, 1872)

We have looked at some of the practical ways of immersing ourselves in nature, but so far we have managed to keep ourselves – the subject of this book – largely away from the lower end of the microscope. No longer.

Physiology students at Imperial College London are taught about circadian rhythms with the help of a rectal thermometer. By measuring their own temperatures over the course of a day, the students learn that our body temperature follows a cycle. From a trough very early in the morning, at about 5 a.m., it rises to a peak about twelve hours later. There is typically a variation between peaks and troughs of 1°c, and although that may not sound massive on first reading, bear in mind that a rise of 1°c is a symptom of influenza.

A fluctuation in body temperature is one of the few straightforward indicators that scientists have been able to use to monitor the roller-coaster of wakefulness and sleepiness that we all experience every day. One thing we all know from our own experience, and which science has confirmed, is that we do not all get on the same ride. Each of us experiences different peaks and troughs of wakefulness each day.

By the time the animal kingdom and plant kingdoms divorced, early in the evolution of life on earth, the genes that enable a sensitivity to the daily cycle of light and dark were already established. They can be found in human DNA, and we share them with other animals and most basic plants to this day. Each time we see the sun set, changes are triggered within us and every living thing around us.

Sleepiness and wakefulness are parts of the physiological ride, but they are not the only things that fluctuate throughout the day. Our individual alertness, mood and energy levels will be influenced by blood sugar, insulin response, allergies, exercise, smells, colours and temperature – and that is before we consider any of the stimulants or sedatives, like caffeine or alcohol, we tend to lob into the system for good measure. In short, the way we feel, and therefore our experience of our surroundings, is shaped by the nature within us.

We are subject to hormonal tides, ones that rise and fall daily, monthly and yearly. Women pick up pheromone cues from other women in their perspiration, and it is this that leads to a synchronization of menstrual cycles in women who live together. With the variations of the hormone cycle, the individual's sense of alertness, wellbeing and mood also changes. There are many women who will assert that a flower does not look equally beautiful at all times of the month. But men will also be fighting upheavals, not least in tidal surges of testosterone. A man who is trying to admire a wildflower with a woman he finds very attractive may have to focus more consciously than the woman. And they might both find a wildflower hard to appreciate at 10 p.m., even under torchlight, as this is the most common time for lovemaking – a consequence of circadian rhythms leading to a particular cultural convention.

We are only keeping step with the rest of the animal kingdom in these habits. Black cats are not lucky between March and May, because this is when mature toms go for a wander in search of a mate and are most likely to be killed crossing a road. Hedgehog road-deaths also peak at this time, with male deaths outnumbering females by a ratio of 2 to 1. Most animals mate at the time of year (indicated by day length) that will lead to birth at a time when food is most prevalent. So the male human testosterone level peaks in October, and the fact foragers are busy in late summer is related – nature has ensured that more babies are born in the late summer months when there is more food around.

Both the man and the woman will find the same species of flower appears subtly different with each passing year, as age shapes us, both through the accumulation of experiences and the natural ageing process. It becomes harder to smell the flower after middle age, and harder to hear the birds around it. Ageing is not all downhill, however, and the Owl of Minerva comes late: wisdom, that hard-to-define quality, gives us an ability to appreciate smaller things with time. The half-scent of a rose may offer a richer experience to an eighty-year-old than the full scent would to a twenty-year-old.

Psychological cycles ride on top of our physiological ones. Our financial or emotional security will influence our experience of the world, and this is true regardless of our situation. The wealthiest person in the world can still hate the world, while the Weyemba people of Sumba in Indonesia feel that their own economic progress has impacted on astronomy: 'the moon rises differently and the sun sets differently now', they believe.

Exercise 14

Imagine a scene: you are looking from halfway up a hill, across a valley, with sunlight reflecting off a meandering river. There are cattle in the fields, and patches of mixed woodland breaking up the pasture. A pink rock stands at the corner of one field. Add a few elements of your own, allow your imagination to fill some blanks. Now hold onto that view.

You are feeling triumphant from a successful walk, and your walking companion has just suggested something that promises an interesting afternoon and possibly evening. You are alert, it is mid-morning, the coffee at breakfast was good and the breakfast was better. You slept well on sheets that had surely been ironed, and you're looking forward to another four days of similar pleasures, during this short walking holiday. Take in the view before you. Pick out each detail. Use the sun to work out the time and the direction you are looking in.

Unfortunately the evening did not go at all as you had hoped. You find yourself walking back up the hill the following morning, alone and on an empty stomach. You need to wash away a sleepless night with fresh air, but you must hurry as you need to head back home much sooner than expected because of serious problems at work. You feel the first annoying heat in your nostrils of a cold coming on. Your muscles are stiff from the day before and one calf muscle feels torn. You reach the same spot and pause. Take in the view before you. How little could you care for the detail? Turn away from the sun and its irritating cheer.

2. The Strengthening Cycle

'The most beautiful emotion we can experience is the mystical. It is the sower of all true art and science. He to whom this emotion is a stranger . . . is as good as dead.'
(ALBERT EINSTEIN)

So far, we have taken the following steps to reconnect with nature:

1. Applied new skills to the natural world, and tried *doing* new things.

2. Flexed our senses and given them a workout.

3. Grown comfortable with landscapes, habitats and the broadest of nature's brushstrokes.

4. Investigated a few of the finer connections to be found.

5. Allowed ourselves to be allured by conflict.

6. Appreciated the role of time in nature, and that we will never get a chance to witness anything in exactly the same way twice.

7. Stepped into the landscape and made ourselves part of the nature experience.

If we do not take the simple steps above, we are gambling a lot on there being another life like this one; if, on the other hand, we do take these steps, then a series of positive consequences follows. Changes occur in how we perceive things, how we think, how we feel and how we act. At this point, the subject becomes a willing object. Nature begins to change us. This positive change encourages us to invest more in the process. The cycle strengthens.

Growing numbers of studies are revealing simple correlations between our exposure to nature, or lack of it, and our wellbeing. Research in the US has shown that the more green spaces in a neighbourhood, the lower the average body mass index of the children who live there.

Many of the health impacts are less well understood, but this is changing. Patients recovering from surgery have been found to need one day less in hospital if trees can be seen from their window instead of just bricks. If pharmaceutical companies could put this effect in a pill, they would do so and they would make billions. But they can't. Nature can't be packaged or marketed easily; we cannot rely on others to sell us a solution.

A recent study has shown that people become more generous after they have seen pictures of nature. Academics like to measure generosity with a basic experimental test called the 'dictator game'. It is very simple: person A is given a sum of money and asked if they would like to give any of it to person B. Studies have shown that if people are being watched, they become more generous, because that is how they wish to be perceived. This effect can even be achieved by putting an image of a pair of eyes on a wall. Amazingly, a picture of flowers has recently been shown to have an even greater impact on human generosity in these experiments than a pair of eyes.

Time spent in nature has been shown to improve self-esteem and conflict resolution. It also reduces absenteeism, and one hour spent in nature can improve memory and attention span by 20 per cent. Nature can calm us, it can help us focus and, for many, it works as an antidepressant. The author Richard Louv has made a convincing case for the power of time spent in nature to improve our relationships with family and friends. Just as families can bond over mutual interests in sport or work, nature can become a shared interest – but it has a particular advantage when it comes to forming bonds: time spent in nature takes us away from impatient and interrupting technology.

Both technology and nature have an allure, and we can find ourselves mesmerized by either. This means that we sometimes have to tug ourselves from one to the other, but once we make the shift there is little or no sense of loss. When we're indoors, such mind-neutral activities as watching TV or checking social media can feel more enticing than putting on a coat and stepping outside. However, after ten minutes in the fresh air these electronic mind-traps lose any magnetism they may once have held.

Instead of castigating computer games as all bad, we might do better to accept that they obviously appeal very strongly to many people, especially the young, and look for lessons within that. One cool sunny October morning following a day of heavy rain, I knew it was a prime time for admiring autumnal fungi in our local woods, and I was very keen to share this with my young sons. They seemed distracted by a computer game at the time, so I decided to fight fire with fire by appealing to their sense of competition and scores. I told them that the record for the greatest number of fungus specimens I'd ever found in one walk was fourteen. We returned two hours later with big grins and a new top score. The boys ran up to their mum and proudly declared that they had found 114 fungi, 100 more than Dad could find on his own. For me that morning also set a different top score: it was among my top ten life experiences to date.

Aside from the relatively easy-to-identify physiological and philosophical benefits, a connection with nature offers something bigger and more mysterious. When we stop to look at something and trace the connection between that organism and ourselves, we invest time in a form of contemplation.

You are walking on limestone hills and you stop to retie your shoelaces. A blister on one foot is rubbing against the sock. You notice beside your foot a plant called a prickly lettuce, and struggle, for fun, to remember the things you have read about it. And then its Latin name comes back to you, *Lactuca serriola*, because this is the plant with serrated edges, which lactates a milky sap if broken. You pause.

The prickly lettuce is absorbing the morning sun. Your eyes are drawn to the sun and it tinkers with your body-clock, making you feel more awake and energetic. The lettuce is thriving in the soil above the limestone. You are thriving by walking on the limestone hills. In a month the flower will be gone; soon you will have left that spot. When you return, the flower may not be there; even if it is, all will be different. The light, colours, scents and temperature will be different. Your feelings, levels of alertness and energy, thoughts, mood and memories will be different. The earth will have revolved a few more times.

There will come a time when the earth continues to turn, the sun rises once more over the limestone hills, but there is no prickly lettuce and there is no you. What little there was of you – beyond a collection of carbon-based chemicals – are the things you have sensed and your reactions to them. And so you stop and look at the lettuce. You glance once more at its leaves and then at the sun. And then you let the lettuce ask you some questions.

'Which direction are you looking in, and what time is it?'

In taking the time to answer these questions you realize that the search takes you to the horizon and then beyond to the earth revolving and orbiting at 19 miles per second. The questions bring you back to the plant, it whispers a suggestion to look at its fellow prickly lettuces. They are all aligned. The prickly lettuce, you remember, has leaves that align north–south. It is flowering, which means it is late summer, and this means the sun has risen north of east. Whilst you are thinking about this, a sundial appears on the dry soil, as the leaves cast a shadow. The sun and flowers give you the understanding that you are looking south on a late summer morning, and invest that understanding with a meaningfulness that would be entirely absent if you were using a watch and compass. A weak sense of connection with time and place begins to form. You feel a surprising joy at this reaction, which fuels a slightly greater curiosity.

Then, to your shock, the lettuce whispers two new questions:

'How are you and who are you?'

You pause, unsure how to answer. Then the plant suggests that the answer to the question will be found in how you perceive your surroundings and how you react to them.

The more we perceive, the greater our chances of discovering something that triggers a reaction. The more connections we notice between the nature we observe, our surroundings and ourselves, the profounder these reactions become. There is a strong correlation between the number of profound reactions we have to the things we notice in life, and the richness of life.

If someone or something surprises, delights, amazes or confounds you, then that is an encounter you will remember. The prickly lettuce, for instance, may be shy at first, but it will do all of these things, if you are curious enough. The harder it is to form a connection with a part of nature, the greater the reward we receive when we finally make that connection.

If our life is made up of perceptions and reactions, then the way we notice and react to a plant or animal helps define who we are. There is nothing original in making a billion dollars or ruling a nation; both have been done a thousand times before by others. The chances are that nobody has ever taken the time to solve the puzzle of how one particular straggly specimen of wild lettuce connects to them as an individual. This unusual line of enquiry will inevitably lead to changes in thought patterns, which will lead to noticing new things, which will subtly alter the way we think and then behave. The result will be originality.

There is a humility that comes with an interest in nature. If it does nothing else, nature can simultaneously excite us by hinting at what we can discover and humble us with our own ignorance. With each passing year this sensation grows. It would be hard to find a record of a person whose deathbed regret was taking too great an interest in their surroundings, although the opposite – regret for failing to fully engage with the world – is widespread and takes many forms.

A combination of humility and aspiration is a trait found in the most interesting of people. Those who choose to reside purely in the practical or philosophical world tend to scorn the land that lies between these two areas, the natural world. But those rare individuals who do things that change the way we think, or think in a way that changes how we behave, have, without exception, understood the insight that a connection with nature can offer.

Investigate any individual who has achieved extraordinary things and a fascination with nature will be found. They will have sought to understand the way the things that fascinate them fit into the broader network. The biggest and boldest ideas are still rooted alongside the plants and animals if we look hard enough. Einstein is best known for his mastery of the mathematical equations that help describe the fundamental physics of the universe, but it should not surprise us that he liked to walk in the Princeton woods each day.

We are all likely to feel a calling at some time in our lives to do something that transcends the ordinary, that goes beyond eating, drinking, reproducing and not shivering. It does not matter what lies at the top of our pyramid, whether it is creative, productive, cerebral, emotional or chaotic . . . Time spent considering nature will help. This is partly because a profound contemplation of *anything* has been proven to help us psychologically, whether it is labelled *meditation, prayer* or *om-shan-ti-ing*. An appreciation of nature enhances both a sense of humility and a fascination with the most ordinary of things. The words of Seneca call out to us from a different millennium: 'It is characteristic of a great soul to scorn great things and prefer what is ordinary.'

Seneca is not alone in believing that people who find things interesting tend to be more interesting people.

Reconnecting with nature is not something that *should* be done. It is not something that we do because it is *good* in itself, or even because it is good for our health. It is a way of finding life more interesting, becoming a more interesting person and then achieving more interesting things.

Time spent considering a prickly lettuce might well help us to achieve the things that we currently consider more important than a lettuce. As you consider this, your mind may be dragged away by a practical need, a hunger that takes you somewhere else. Hunger will take you to the first steps of Maslow's pyramid. What will happen if you bend down and pick some young leaves from the prickly lettuce to eat?

Your first reaction will be that the leaves taste quite bitter, but not wholly unpleasant. If your hunger drives you on to eat more, you may suddenly notice that the pain from your blister has evaporated and you have begun to feel relaxed and even a little sleepy. The plant contains lactucarium, which is a mild sedative and painkiller and has been used as an alternative to opium. As you lie down in your weak opiate daze, it occurs to you that this weed that few would notice has been your compass, your calendar, your clock, your grocer, your etymological teaser, your pharmacist and now your quiet companion.

We are what we eat, but nature offers us more than just food for our stomachs. It feeds us thoughts and ideas that help take us wherever we want to go. Nature suggests fascinating new paths for each of us – sometimes after a good sleep in the sun.

3. There Are Only Two People Outside

'"Miracles have ceased." Have they indeed? When?
They had not ceased this afternoon when I walked into
the wood and got into bright, miraculous sunshine,
in shelter from the roaring wind.'
(Ralph Waldo Emerson)

Anyone who follows the steps set out in this book will begin to reconnect with nature. This will lead to experiences that surprise and delight in small and then bigger ways. These experiences feed a desire to invest more in the process. New skills are learned, new knowledge gained, senses are heightened, awareness grows, new connections are discovered and experiences become more profound. The cycle strengthens further.

Enriching our experience of the outdoors will make us appreciate how unaware most of us are, most of the time. This is both worrying and exciting, and leads to a parting between the connected person and the disconnected. To the aware, there is no point in occupying a middle ground, as it merely offers a weaker, less satisfying version of what is available. The gulf grows as the aware person takes more delight in the process, and their sense of connection flourishes.

It does not take long before it is possible to look back at your former self – the person who did not connect with nature – and find a strange creature you barely recognize. Instead of pitying this poor mole, one that has never taken the time to sniff above the ground, you will want to encourage others to explore, to poke their snouts into the air and not to fear the million scents they find there.

A Final Exercise

Once you have read this book and tried the exercises, return to a spot you knew before reading the book. Ask yourself the following questions:

1. What time is it?
2. What direction am I looking?

Use nature to answer these questions. Then ask yourself two more:

3. Is this place the same place I stood in before?
4. Am I the same person who was here earlier?

There are no right answers to questions three and four, and it is the process of trying to reach an answer of any kind that is of value. Even if there were correct answers, they would have changed by the time you arrived at them.

A Final Thought

It should be expected that we will find wonder in a vast mountain landscape, but it is a more serious challenge to find wonder in a hill. It is a great achievement to find it in a molehill.

Homework

This book is a fusion of my experiences with nature, formed since childhood, and a fifteen-year fascination with natural navigation, as well as the work of those whose writing has inspired me. I hope you will find much to inspire you in this book, and in the following ones too.

My second book, *The Natural Explorer* (Sceptre, 2012), expands on many of the themes in this book and also introduces a few new ones.

The following books have been valuable sources. They are all recommended further reading.

II. The Ground Ahead

1. Getting Ready

The New Times Nature Diary, by Derwent May (Robson, 1995), is a beautifully written and illustrated collection of nature observations. It offers an excellent introduction to noticing change in nature.

III. Finding a Path

1. *A Practical Way In*

For a guide to natural navigation, my own book *The Natural Navigator* (Virgin, 2010) offers a thorough tour of the subject and is a good place to start. You may also find useful *How to Find Your Way Without Map or Compass*, by Harold Gatty (Dover, 2003).

When it comes to practical advice on foraging, *The Forager's Handbook* by Miles Irving (Ebury, 2009), is well written, well produced and comprehensive. Another excellent book is *Food for Free*, by Richard Mabey (HarperCollins, 1992). This modern classic has helped trigger a renaissance in an atrophying skill.

Tom Brown, Jr has written many good books on the subject of tracking. The one that complements the approach of this book best is *Tom Brown's Field Guide to Nature Observation and Tracking* (Berkley Books, 1983).

Teachers and parents will find lots of inspiration in *Sharing Nature with Children*, by Joseph Cornell (Dawn Publications, 1998). It describes itself as 'The Classic Parents' and Teachers' Nature Awareness Guidebook', which seems about right to me.

2. *The Senses*

Connecting Into Observation and Awareness, by Jon Boyd (Amethyst Moon, 2007), is a little-known book, but worth searching out for an eclectic mixture of orthodox and unusual ways of sensing the outdoors.

Coyote's Guide to Connecting With Nature, by Jon Young, Ellen Haas and Evan McGown (OWLink Media, 2010), is a big book with an unusual approach. Like this book, it is written by those with experience of teaching outdoors, and this shines through. It contains many activities that will help further your connection.

David Chamovitz's superb book, *What a Plant Knows* (Oneworld, 2012), is perfect for anyone who wishes to learn more about what plants can sense and how they react.

3. The Big Relationships

A Sand County Almanac, by Aldo Leopold (Oxford University Press, 1968) is regarded as a classic, and rightly so. By taking a passionate, practical and entertaining look at his local environment, Leopold demonstrates that it is not the detail that we find that makes a nature experience, but our approach. This book helped shape the environmental movement by eloquently proposing that anything that goes against the beauty or stability of an area is wrong. More subtly, it is an archetype for two nature philosophies: look and you will find; do and you will learn.

4. The Finer Connections

Biophilia, by Edward O. Wilson (Harvard College, 1984), is another classic by a giant in the field of the human–nature relationship.

5. *The Beauty of Conflict*

The Botany of Desire, by Michael Pollan (Bloomsbury, 2013), is a book that recasts the plant as the subject of the nature story.

IV. Getting Closer

1. *Hidden Calendars*

The Country Diaries, edited by Alan Taylor (Canongate Books, 2010), is one of the best compendiums of historical and contemporary rural anecdote that I have come across.

The Morville Year, by Katherine Swift (Bloomsbury, 2011), is the best gardening book I have read. By looking at her garden over the course of a year, Swift gives us the opportunity to see seasonal change through the eyes of a passionate expert on her patch.

Wild Hares and Humming Birds, by Stephen Moss (Square Peg, 2011), is a very enjoyable view of an English village, seen through an expert naturalist's eyes over the course of the year.

2. *Fast Change*

Pip Pip, by Jay Griffiths (Flamingo, 1999), is a beautiful collection of stories that will help any reader to reconnect with time in a more fundamental way.

V. Real Connection

1. *The Clocks Within*

Rhythms of Life, by Russell Foster and Leon Kreitzman (Profile, 2004), is a thorough yet accessible book about biological clocks.

2. *The Strengthening Cycle*

The Nature Principle, by Richard Louv (Algonquin, 2012), is an excellent book that deserves to be read very widely. Louv does an impressive job of setting out the benefits of a life that includes nature-immersion, in the face of a ubiquitous digital onslaught. It has provided many useful examples.

Embracing the Ordinary, by Michael Foley (Simon & Schuster, 2012), is not a nature book as such, but it is a very good book that shares the philosophy of deriving great pleasure from small things.

3. *There Are Only Two People Outside*

There are no books that are of specific relevance to this chapter. The most relevant one would be your own diary or blog, if you keep one. You may not notice changes in your perspective over the course of a day or a week, but if you revisit the steps and ideas in this book over a year then comparisons should prove interesting.

Your desire to see will grow noticeably, and you may spot many new things. But the real change will come often not because of the more interesting things that you see, but because you will have learned how to find more interest in the things you do see.

Picture Acknowledgements

The author and publisher would like to thank the following for permission to reproduce the images used in this book:

Page 27 Stinging nettles © Kathy Collins / Getty Images

Pages 32–33 Mares' tails © S. J. Krasemann / Photolibrary / Getty Images

Page 43 Crescent moon © Amy White & Al Petteway / National Geographic / Getty Images

Page 69 Mountain © Ken Canning / Getty Images

Page 81 Finding the North Star © Ruth Murray

Page 83 Ghost orchid © Photoshot / TIPS

Page 85 Emperor penguin © Paul Nicklen / National Geographic / Getty Images

Page 85 Cassowary © Karl Lehmann / Lonely Planet Images / Getty Images

Page 93 Firing range © Photoshot

Pages 96–97 Giraffe © Britta Kasholm-Tengve / Getty Images

Page 108–109 The Ring of Brodgar at sunset, Orkney, Scotland © Iain Sarjeant / Oxford Scientific / Getty Images

Page 112 Conifer tree © Ruth Murray

Page 115 Daisies © Ian Graham / Getty Images

All other images provided courtesy of the author.

Notes

Notes

Notes

Notes

TOOLS FOR THINKING

A NEW RANGE OF NOTEBOOKS, PENCILS, CARDS
& GIFTS FROM THE SCHOOL OF LIFE

Good thinking requires good tools. To complement our classes, books and therapies, THE SCHOOL OF LIFE now offers a range of stationery products and gifts that are both highly useful and stimulating for the eye and mind.

If you enjoyed this book, we'd encourage you to check out other titles in the series:

If you'd like to explore more good ideas for everyday life, THE SCHOOL OF LIFE runs a regular programme of classes, weekends, secular sermons and events in London and other cities around the world.

Browse our shop and visit:

THESCHOOLOFLIFE.COM
TWITTER.COM/THESCHOOLOFLIFE

panmacmillan.com
twitter.com/panmacmillan